D1234468

In honour of J. D. Douglas (1922–2003)
and John R. W. Stott (1921–2011)
who laid the foundations for The Lausanne Library.

THE THIRD LAUSANNE CONGRESS ON WORLD EVANGELIZATION

CHRIST OUR RECONCILER
GOSPEL • CHURCH • WORLD

EDITED BY **JULIA E. M. CAMERON**

The Third Lausanne Congress on World Evangelization
was held in collaboration with the World Evangelical Alliance.

IVP Books
An imprint of InterVarsity Press
Downers Grove, Illinois

InterVarsity Press
P.O. Box 1400, Downers Grove, IL 60515-1426
World Wide Web: www.ivpress.com
E-mail: email@ivpress.com

InterVarsity Press® is the book-publishing division of InterVarsity Christian Fellowship/USA®, a movement of students and faculty active on campus at hundreds of universities, colleges and schools of nursing in the United States of America, and a member movement of the International Fellowship of Evangelical Students. For information about local and regional activities, write Public Relations Dept., InterVarsity Christian Fellowship/USA, 6400 Schroeder Rd., P.O. Box 7895, Madison, WI 53707-7895, or visit the IVCF website at <www.intervarsity.org>.

Bible Versions

The Holy Bible, New International Version®. NIV®. *Copyright ©1973, 1978, 1984 by International Bible Society. Used by permission of Zondervan Publishing House. All rights reserved.*

The Holy Bible, English Standard Version, *copyright © 2001 by Crossway Bibles, a division of Good News Publishers. Used by permission. All rights reserved.*

The New King James Version. *Copyright © 1982 by Thomas Nelson, Inc. Used by permission.*

The poem on pp. 141-42 is "God in the Common Place" by Jim Elliot, published in The Journal of Jim Elliot *(ed. Elisabeth Elliot) by Revell, a division of Baker Publishing Group (2007), p. 106. Used by permission.*

Design: Cindy Kiple
Images: © 2010 The Lausanne Movement, www.lausanne.org, All Rights Reserved

ISBN 978-0-8308-3776-2

Printed in the United States of America ∞

Library of Congress Cataloging-in-Publication Data

Christ our reconciler : Gospel, church, world / Julia Cameron, ed.
    p. cm.
  Includes bibliographical references.
  ISBN 978-0-8308-3776-2 (pbk. : alk. paper)
  1. International Congress on World Evangelization (3rd : 2010 : Cape Town, South Africa) 2. Lausanne Committee for World Evangelization. 3. Evangelistic work—Congresses. 4. Evangelicalism—Congresses. 5. Missions—Congresses. I. Cameron, Julia.
BV3755.C49 2012
266—dc23

                                                                    2012027649

P 18 17 16 15 14 13 12 11 10 9 8 7 6 5 4 3 2 1

Y 27 26 25 24 23 22 21 20 19 18 17 16 15 14 13 12

CONTENTS

THE LAUSANNE MOVEMENT

The Lausanne Movement was founded following the 1974 Congress on World Evangelization, held in Lausanne, Switzerland. This Congress was convened by the evangelist Billy Graham.

Lausanne is a network of evangelical leaders, thinkers and reflective practitioners. Its purpose is to strengthen the church for world evangelization. To this end, it serves the body of Christ as a *catalyst* for engaging major issues by:

- *Connecting and convening evangelical leaders* (in Christian ministry, and in the secular professions) for focused discussion, prayer and strategic action on issues which impact the church and God's world;
- *Communicating ideas and strategy* by, for example, publishing books and occasional papers (hard copy and online), and using social media and targeted communication to inform, persuade and stimulate ideas and action;
- *Hosting discussion and resource sharing* through the online Lausanne Global Conversation, which provides a forum for ideas and strategy on mission and evangelization.

The Third Lausanne Congress on World Evangelization (Cape Town 2010) brought together more than 4,000 participants from 198 countries. *The Cape Town Commitment*, issuing from this Congress, stands in the historic line of *The Lausanne Covenant* (1974) and *The Manila Manifesto* (1989). It opens with a Confession of Faith, framed in the language of covenantal love, followed by a Call to Action. Its Call to Action reflects the voices of all who participated in Congress discussions, in a genuine desire to hear the voice of the Holy Spirit. *The Cape Town Commitment* forms the basis for Lausanne's priorities.

The Lausanne Movement is anchored by its Theology Working Group, originally established under the leadership of John Stott, who served as chief architect of *The Lausanne Covenant*. In addition, it has Working Groups on Strategy, Intercession and Communications.

'The spirit of Lausanne'

The phrase 'the spirit of Lausanne' arose out of the 1974 Congress. It captures the Movement's ideals: dedication to prayer, and to the study of God's Word; a desire to work in unity and partnership; a clear reflection of the hope of the gospel; and humility in service.

To learn more, and to join the Lausanne Global Conversation on mission and evangelization, go to www.lausanne.org or email info@lausanne.org.

FOREWORD

Christ our Reconciler has entrusted to us the message of reconciliation. We, his church on earth, bear a glorious task and a serious responsibility. His command to make disciples of all nations has never been rescinded; it is this command which gave rise to The Lausanne Movement following the 1974 Congress on World Evangelization in Lausanne, Switzerland, and remains its lifeblood.

In every generation we need to understand our times, as the men of Issachar understood theirs.[1] Only through the dedicated hard work of studying Scripture, and studying the world around us, will we, like those men from Issachar, 'know what to do'.

John Stott loved to remind us that Christ gave gifts to the church to *share*. He referred to The Lausanne Movement rather beautifully as 'an exchange of gifts'. We offer this book as a gift from the church on all continents to the church in your nation. May it be a means of enriching one another in our grasp of Scripture, and in our love of Christ.

The purpose of The Third Lausanne Congress was to strengthen the church for world evangelization. To this end we were joined on-site by participants from 198 nations, selected from local churches, agencies, national and international movements, and including senior leaders in the public arenas. Through our GlobaLink we were able to extend our discussions; we had over 600 registered remote sites in some ninety countries. We received interactive responses from GlobaLink, and from television and radio programmes created on-site, through our blogger network, and from news reports filed by nearly a hundred reporters and crew. Our aim? To discern what the Holy Spirit is saying to the churches now, and the outcome of our work is contained in *The Cape Town Commitment*. I would urge you, your church, your student fellowship on campus, your Christian fellowship at the office or in the lab, to study it carefully before God, and to find your place in its outworking.[2]

All good planning needs a clear grasp of where we are now, and of where we want to be. More than that, it needs a shrewd sense of external factors which bear on our plans, and the right people to take those plans forward. In this regard, we do not forget our brothers and sisters in lands where there is persecution, and for whom any forward planning for the gospel is very costly. We trust this book will engage with all aspects of planning, and stimulate robust discussion among leaders of churches and agencies. We trust too that its principles will serve 'the church at large': Christians in the workplace, in fields of government, business, academia, industry, medicine and the media. In offering this volume, we have no vaunted ideas of ourselves; we work simply as servants.

I want to express gratitude to Blair Carlson, Congress Director, who served for many years with the Billy Graham Evangelistic Association. I also want to thank Ramez Atallah, Director of the Bible Society of Egypt, who chaired the Programme Committee, his co-chair Mark Marlowe (USA), and Grace Mathews (India) who served as Programme Director. They were assisted by a fine team in building a programme and a speaker list which drew some of the best evangelical thinkers and most courageous practitioners from the global church. We can offer only a limited selection of the programme in a single volume; you will find much more on the website.

The international Board overseeing the development of the Congress drew on the wisdom of good friends who prayed for us. I think, for example, of Dr Billy Graham, founder of The Lausanne Movement; of John Stott, who served as Honorary Chair until his death in 2011; and of the late James Hudson Taylor III, whose knowledge of the Chinese church was second to none; of Prof Samuel Escobar and Dr René Padilla from Latin America, names synonymous with Lausanne since the 1974 Congress; and of Archbishop Henry Luke Orombi from Uganda, who served as Honorary Chair of the Africa Host Committee.

My purpose is not to list names, for that would fill many pages. It is to reflect the global nature of the Congress, and in so doing to express something of the burden we now feel, as recipients and stewards of rich gifts brought to the table by Christian leaders from many nations.

The apostle Paul had a passionate plea: that those in the church grow up into 'the measure of the stature of the fullness of Christ'. May this book be a small contribution to that growth.

S. Douglas Birdsall
Executive Chair, The Lausanne Movement
Boston, Massachusetts
January 2012

BILLY GRAHAM

MONTREAT, NORTH CAROLINA 28707

My dear Brothers and Sisters in Christ

Greetings in the name of our Lord Jesus Christ to all of you who have gathered in Cape Town for this historic conference! Although I am unable to be with you in person, I want to assure you that I will be praying daily for you.

In 1974, twenty-seven hundred participants from 151 countries came together for the first Lausanne conference. The world has changed greatly since then – politically, economically, technologically, demographically, and even religiously. One of your tasks during Cape Town 2010 will be to analyse those changes, and to assess their impact on the mission to which God has called us in this generation.

But in all your deliberations, I pray you may never forget that some things have not changed in the last 36 years – nor will they ever change until our Lord returns. For one thing, the deepest needs of the human heart have not changed: the need to be reconciled to God, and to experience His love and forgiveness and transforming power. Nor has the Gospel changed: the Good News that God loves us and sent His only Son, Jesus Christ, into the world to forgive us and save us by His death and resurrection. Nor has Christ's command to His disciples changed: the mandate to go into all the world and proclaim the Gospel, urging men and women everywhere to put their faith and trust in Jesus Christ as Savior and Lord.

I am praying that, during your time in Cape Town, the Holy Spirit will not only continue what has been done in previous conferences, but that He will increase your burden for a lost and dying world, and cause you to rededicate yourself to the priority and urgency of evangelism. May He also encourage you and refresh you as you gather together in Bible study, prayer and fellowship. As you leave

Cape Town, may you go with a renewed commitment to live for Christ, and a fresh determination to walk humbly with Him every day. Never lose sight of your calling, but keep your eyes on Christ every day, as you take time to be with Him in prayer and personal Bible study.

May God bless each of you – and may He bless our world because of what He does in your lives during these days.

Your brother in Christ.

John Stott
12 Weymouth Street
LONDON W1W 5BY

Dear Brothers and Sisters in Christ

Owing to my ill health, I shall be very sorry to miss you in Cape Town in October. But I will be with you all each day in prayer, expectation and confidence, as you plan to make known the uniqueness of Jesus Christ all over the world.

I have been thanking God all through the years since 1974 for the growth of The Lausanne Movement and how God has used it for his own glory. Even more, however, I thank God for the growth of the worldwide church in those years, especially in the great continents of the majority world.

For that reason, I rejoice that this Congress is being hosted in Africa, and I pray that you will be able to share richly in the blessing God has poured out on the church in that continent, as well as sharing in the pain and suffering of his people there.

As you will be studying Ephesians together, my encouragement to you echoes that of the apostle Paul:

> I urge you to live a life worthy of the calling you have received. Be completely humble and gentle; be patient, bearing with one another in love. Make every effort to keep the unity of the Spirit through the bond of peace.

John Stott

Honorary Chairman, The Lausanne Movement[1]

DAY 1

TRUTH: Making the case for the truth of Christ in our pluralistic and globalized world

TESTIMONY:
'I KNOW THE GOSPEL IS TRUE'
Gyeong Ju Son (North Korea)

Gyeong Ju Son, wearing her school uniform, came onto the stage accompanied by her pastor. She stepped up to the microphone with poise, and with a deep conviction of the truth of the gospel. Her story, redolent with faith, quickly circulated through social media and became one of the most-viewed presentations in the Congress.

Hello. My name is Gyeong Ju Son. I was born in Pyongyang, the capital of North Korea. I came to South Korea in 2009. I am eighteen years old and I am currently in my second year of high school.

I was the only child of a very wealthy family. My father was an assistant of Kim Jong-Il, who was the leader of North Korea. When I was only six years old, my family was politically persecuted by the North Korean government, so we escaped to China. That was in 1998.

After we settled in China, one of our relatives led my family to church. There my parents came to know the amazing grace and love of God. Then only a few months later, my mother, who was pregnant with her second child, passed away with leukaemia. Yet in the midst of this family tragedy, my father started a Bible study with the missionaries from South Korea and America. It was his strong desire to become a missionary to North Korea. But suddenly in 2001, he was reported and arrested by the Chinese police and sent back to North Korea, where he was sentenced to prison. He was forced to leave me behind.

But the three years he served in prison only made my father's faith stronger. He cried out to God more desperately, rather than complaining or blaming him. When he was released from prison, he returned to China. We were reunited briefly. It was then that he started to gather Bibles, not long after he had decided to return to North Korea to share Christ's message of life and hope among the hopeless people of his homeland. He chose not to go to South Korea where he could have enjoyed religious freedom. Instead, he chose to return to North Korea to share the love of God in that dangerous land.

It breaks my heart to tell you that in 2006 his work was discovered by the North Korean government and he was again imprisoned. I have heard no word from my father nor about him ever since. In all probability, he has been shot dead in public on charges of treason and espionage, as is so often the case for persecuted Christians in North Korea.

When my father was first arrested in 2001 and forced to leave me and return to North Korea, I was not yet a Christian. That was when I was adopted by a young Chinese pastor's family. They showed me great love and care. Through them, God protected me. But the pastor and his wife had to go to America in 2007. Shortly after that, I was given the opportunity to go to South Korea. That was while I was still in China, staying at the Korean Consulate in Beijing waiting to come to South Korea.

Late one night, I saw Jesus in a dream. He had tears in his eyes. He walked towards me and said, 'Gyeong Ju, how much longer are you going to keep me waiting? Walk with me. Yes, you lost your earthly father, but I am your heavenly Father, and whatever has happened to you was because I love you.'

After I woke up from the dream, I knelt and prayed to God for the first time. That night I realized that God, my Father, loves me and cares about me so very much that he sent his Son, Jesus, to die for me. I prayed, 'God, here I am. I just lay down everything and give you my heart, my soul, my mind and my strength. Please use me as you will.'

Now God has placed deep in my heart a great love for North Korea, just as my father was used there for God's kingdom. I now desire to be obedient to God. I want to bring the love of Jesus to North Korea. I look back over my short life and I see God's hand everywhere. Six years in North Korea, eleven years in China, and the time spent here in South Korea. Everything I suffered, all the sadness and grief, everything that I experienced and learned, I want to give it all to God and use my life for his kingdom. I hope to honour my father and to bring glory to my heavenly Father by serving God with my whole heart.

Currently I'm working hard to get into university to study political science and diplomacy. Then I want to work for the people of North Korea, whose rights have been taken away. I believe God's heart cries out for the lost people of North Korea. I humbly ask you, my brothers and sisters here in this place, to have the same heart of God.

Please pray that the same light of God's grace and mercy that reaches my father and my mother, and now me, will one day descend upon the people of North Korea, my people. Thank you.

EPHESIANS 1
Ajith Fernando (Sri Lanka)

The first chapter of Ephesians is a rich passage containing much vital, foundational material and beautiful truths. The apostle Paul launches in with passion. After his customary greeting, he moves into one single sentence of doxology (praise), spanning twelve verses (verses 3–14), with 202 words in the Greek.

Verse 3 is rich in blessing, with three words carrying this sense of blessing, all derived from the same root: 'Blessed be the God and Father of our Lord Jesus Christ, who has blessed us in Christ with every spiritual blessing in the heavenly places.' All we need for an abundant life is here, in what God has done in Christ. The praise delves deeper and deeper into the nature of our salvation.

Chosen by God (1:4–6)

We were chosen before the foundation of the world and predestined by God, for three reasons:

- 'That we should be holy' (verse 4)
- That we might be adopted as children through Jesus Christ according to the purpose of God's will (verse 5)
- That all this should be 'to the praise of his glorious grace, with which he has blessed us in the Beloved' (verse 6)

So our salvation is all God's doing and based on what Christ has done for us. In *The Genius of Grace*, Sam Gordon tells the story of a boy who was asked, 'Have you found Jesus?' He thought for a moment and replied, 'Sir, I didn't know Jesus was lost. But I do know that when I was lost, he found me.'

Four great salvation words (1:7–8)

Here we see how salvation was won for us: 'In him we have redemption through his blood, the forgiveness of our trespasses, according to the riches of his grace, which he lavished upon us, in all wisdom and insight.' Note the four great words of the doctrine of salvation. First *redemption,* a picture from the market place, pointing to the price paid for our freedom. Then *blood,* the most common word in the New Testament to describe the death of Christ, carrying the idea of life violently taken. Then *forgiveness* of trespasses, the result of salvation. Finally *grace,* 'lavished' upon us, suggesting overflow, to drive home the truth that God's grace is greater than our sin. If verses 4–6 showed us that our individual salvation is entirely God's initiative, then verses 7–8 describe the work God did to win our salvation, a series of events enacted in Christ Jesus to give us a comprehensive salvation.

The mystery of God's plan for the world (1:9–10)

Grace came 'in all wisdom and insight' (verse 8). 'Mystery' is the word Paul chooses to describe the great truths once hidden and now revealed in the gospel. The great wisdom of God has provided a way to save humanity. This great gospel, which the world was waiting for eagerly, is now a reality. Verse 10 shows that this mystery has a future aspect. It is 'a plan for the fullness of time, to unite all things in him, things in heaven and things on earth'. The gospel is cosmic in scope. We are awaiting the total triumph of God when everything in creation will be consciously under God.

All this has implications for us. Most people come to Christ because they see him meet a personal need. But this is only a fraction of the truth of the gospel. People who come to Christ in this way may simply see the God of the Bible as stronger than their gods, and transfer their other ideas about god to this new God. But their thoughts of God need to be *transformed,* not simply transferred. They must come to realize that they have entered into a kingdom which is marching towards total victory, which was won by earth-shattering historic events.

The gospel is deeper, fuller and grander than a God who meets immediate needs. When people find that some needs are not met, they can easily leave the church and go elsewhere for help. We see far too much of this. From my life's ministry with first-generation Christians, I conclude that people *come to* Christ because he meets a need, but they *stay* with Christ once they realize he is the Truth. Once they come, we must teach them the *whole* truth of God's plan of salvation.

I was one of the preachers at a three-hour service on Good Friday. We sang a lot of songs between the seven messages, all focused on the subjective appeal of the cross – how much Jesus had suffered to save us, and how we must respond to his love. Not one song described how our salvation was achieved at the cross. But that is the focus in the biblical narrative of the death of Christ. We tend to focus on what people like to hear, but neglect what people should hear.

People find the objective realities of the work of Christ difficult to grasp (and it was difficult in the first century too): how we are redeemed from sin; how Jesus could bear the wrath of God on our behalf; how his blood can cleanse us from all sin; and how we are justified because he bore our guilt. To help us, the Bible uses numerous pictures to bring out different facets. But because it is difficult to understand, many Christians focus only on aspects that people do understand. This has to change if our generation is to understand, and pass down, the meaning of the greatest thing about the gospel – the work of Christ for our salvation.

God's plan will culminate in total victory. There is such security in knowing our salvation is something God initiated and did a huge work to win! It does not depend upon our performance, but on God's work in us. There is such security in knowing we belong to a movement headed for ultimate conquest over evil and the restoration of the whole universe! When we are troubled by our frailties and by severe trials and persecutions, we will not give up, because we know that Jesus is with us, and his triumph will be complete.

We urgently need to return in our teaching and preaching to an explanation of the nature of salvation, and to what God has done to make it complete, and to the fact that we are moving towards Christ's total victory over everything.

For the praise of God's glory (1:11–12)

Our salvation was a result of God's predestination (verse 11). Verse 12 reinforces verse 6. Our predestination results in the praise of God's glorious *grace*; our salvation results in the praise of God's *glory*. When people see us, they should notice the amazing grace that has resulted in this marvellous work in us, and praise the God who initiated this grace.

Many nations have small Christian communities, and people come little by little into God's family. We long for the day when nations will sit up and take note of the gospel. This will happen when they see Christians reflecting the nature of God in their behaviour. Those tired of corruption will find that Christians do not resort to corruption. Those tired of the individualism that alienates will find true community in the church, and the lonely will discover true companionship and sacrificial concern.

> Let us not be satisfied with a trickle of people coming to Christ.

Those tired of injustice will find that Christians uphold justice and help bring others to experience it. Then people might become enamoured in a fresh way with Jesus Christ.

One reason for the conversion of the Roman Empire in the third century AD was that Christians lived holy and loving lives which attracted people to Jesus. In Sri Lanka after the Boxing Day tsunami hit, we saw a little of what can happen when Christians are at the forefront of relief. Let us not be satisfied with a trickle of people coming to Christ in our nations. Let us dream of, and work for, the day when whole nations are attracted to him because they see God's glorious grace at work in us.

How we are saved and preserved (1:13–14)

Paul rounds off his doxology with two more aspects of our glorious salvation. He emphasizes that the Ephesians were saved after they heard the word of truth and believed in Jesus: 'In him you also, when you heard the word of truth, the gospel of your salvation, and believed in him . . . ' (verse 13a). We spread the gospel because we believe the Creator has given truth which saves. Jesus claimed to *be* the Truth (John 14:6), the only way to the Father, and we can believe this great claim because he is equal with God. This message is from the Creator of all humans, so it must be given to all humans.

Recently there has been a shying away from proclamation evangelism. Some say that people can be saved without hearing the gospel. Now we do not want to dictate to God whom he must save. But the Bible is clear that the only hope for people is to hear the Word and believe the gospel. Many people quote a statement attributed to St Francis of Assisi, that we should witness using all means and use words only if necessary, thereby downplaying the importance of verbal witness. There is some question as to whether St Francis ever made this statement. But even if he did, he himself used words all the time as he sought to bring people to God.

When we realize that people are eternally lost without Christ, we will see evangelism as an urgent and serious obligation. We can find ourselves involved in so many things, so that we neglect the task of proclaiming the good news to lost people. This is a temptation we must constantly overcome; other things will always be more esteemed.

Paul uses two metaphors to show how the Holy Spirit helps us. *First*, we 'were sealed with the promised Holy Spirit' (verse 13b), as a letter in those days would have borne the seal of its sender. Having the Holy Spirit in our lives is a sign to us that we belong to God. *Secondly*, the Holy Spirit is described as 'the guarantee of our inheritance', until we acquire possession of it, 'to the praise of his glory'. When making a purchase, such as a piece of land, buyers make a down payment to assure the seller that they will buy it. When we know that the Holy Spirit is with us, that gives us assurance that there is a place reserved for us in the heavenly kingdom.

There has been a tendency when talking about assurance to focus only on the biblical text. This is certainly the most important way to be sure of our salvation. The Bible says clearly that those who believe will be saved. We were taught that, first come the facts, then faith in those facts, and only after these our feelings. Look at the description in verses 13 and 14 of the assurance that comes through experiencing the Holy Spirit. Perhaps in this postmodern era, with its special emphasis on experience, an experiential case for the assurance of salvation should get more prominence.

Thanksgiving and a request (1:15–23)

Paul's second sentence spans nine verses, as he describes how he prays for the Ephesians. In typical style, it includes thanksgiving and petition.

Thanksgiving: for faith and love (1:15–16)

Paul thanks God for the Ephesians' faith in the Lord Jesus and their love toward all the saints. Faith is mentioned in seven phrases, and love in five. Of the five times love is mentioned, four specify that it is love for the saints – all the saints. The radical individualism of our cultures has infected us Christians too. Often we think of Christianity simply in terms of our own obedience to God. In our definition of obedience, we do not include our relationship with fellow Christians, let alone *all* Christians. We pick and choose our friends, and ignore other Christians. Ephesians is a book about the church, and right at the start we learn a major aspect of what it means to be a church: Christians love one another, and are committed to one another.

The loss of commitment in the world today has resulted in a lot of lonely people. Our answer to that runs against our culture; costly commitment is very inconvenient. Yet through that commitment comes a richness of experience, which is what the world is looking for. When people get tired of individualism, may they find Christians daring to practise community. May they say, as they said of the early Christians, 'See how they love one another.'

A request: for knowledge of Christian hope and power (1:17–23)

Paul describes what he prays for the Ephesian church (verse 17): essentially that they will have a greater knowledge of God. He highlights two aspects of this knowledge: that they may know 'the hope

to which he has called [them]', and 'the riches of his glorious inheritance in the saints' (verse 18).

Unjust rulers misused the hope of heaven to lull people into
accepting injustice on earth, and sometimes Christians were overwhelmed under unjust burdens. But hope is part of the gospel. The
verb and the noun occur fifty-five times in Paul's epistles. What is
this future blessing for which we hope? It is 'the riches of his glorious
inheritance in the saints'. Paul had riches that could not be spoiled
by tough earthly circumstances; his wealth depended on his standing
before God.

Paul says we are God's glorious inheritance. Our greatest wealth
is that the God who owns the cattle on a thousand hills considers us as his inheritance. This hope will be fully realized only in
heaven. But the thought that God
views us as a precious treasure is
already a source of great joy. Even Paul
who is in prison is like a millionaire. A
man once told his wife, 'One day we
will be rich and we can buy a lot of things.' His wife answered,
'We are already rich; maybe one day we will have more money so
that we can buy *more* things.' She had grasped this truth. When God
is with us and we know that he delights in us, then as the Bible tells
us, we will be joyous people. And joy is the greatest wealth we can
have on earth.

**Joy is the greatest
wealth we can
have on earth.**

Next Paul prays that they may know 'what is the immeasurable
greatness of his power toward us who believe, according to the
working of his great might' (verse 19). Paul uses different ways to
highlight the greatness of God's power available to us: 'immeasurable greatness', 'according to the working of his great might'. Then
he talks of the unleashing of God's power in Christ's resurrection,
exaltation and conquest over every spiritual power of evil. Again he
uses vivid language to describe this victory:

that he worked in Christ when he raised him from the dead and
seated him at his right hand in the heavenly places, far above all

rule and authority and power and dominion, and above every name that is named, not only in this age but also in the one to come. And he put all things under his feet and gave him as head over all things to the church.

(verses 20–22)

All these great victories of Christ are for the benefit of the church. For us!

We have wealth in the hope of knowing that we are God's inheritance. Because it is hope, it will not be fully realized until we are in heaven. Yet even on earth, we are rich people. We have power, won for us through the resurrection, exaltation and conquest of Christ. This power will turn everything into good for us, just as it turned the tragedy of the cross to the triumph of the resurrection.

There is a corrective here to the prosperity teaching sweeping the church. Yes, we have power to triumph in all circumstances. But we must leave room for the glorious anticipation of hope. By looking for wealth here and now, we can lose sight of the greatest wealth of all, which is hope – seeing beyond the present troubles to the bright future God has in store for us. Sometimes that power is made perfect when we are weak on earth. Paul discovered this when he prayed to be delivered from his thorn in the flesh. He was a poor man in prison when he wrote to the Ephesians. But he was a rich man with the wealth of the hope to which he was called. Our final rewards will be in heaven. But on earth, amid the hardship, we have power to live victoriously.

Amid the hardship, we have power to live victoriously.

Even in prison, Paul was overwhelmed by his wealth as a Christian. How he longs for the Ephesian Christians to know this! So he prays that the eyes of their hearts would be enlightened (verse 18). They could be spiritually blinded by sin or unbelief or hopelessness and not see their riches. What if the world sees us deprived of our freedoms, and persecuted for our beliefs, but as richer than the richest people on earth? Then they would see that Christ is the source of true riches, the kind of riches they need. If God calls us to go to prison so that the world may see how rich the gospel is, may we gladly go!

Paul was excited about this gospel. Look at the words he uses. Mystery that the world has been waiting for. Grace that is lavished on us. Rich, glorious, powerful, immeasurable greatness, true might. And this is the message that we give to the world, a glorious message. Paul was clearly consumed by the gospel. The day we lose the wonder of the gospel, we lose focus. Paul exulted in the gospel, and we can do the same.

Ajith Fernando, author and speaker, is former National Director and now Teaching Director of Sri Lanka Youth for Christ; he is a senior advisor to the Lausanne Theology Working Group. www.ajithfernando.org

TRUTH MATTERS
Carver T. Yu (Hong Kong)

Truth, as embodied in the Scriptures and the person of Christ, is the foundation of all knowledge.[1]

We in Asia have lived for centuries with the reality of cultural and religious plurality. Diversity is part of life in Asia. Respectful and sensitive to others, we live by and large in harmony; inoffensive but firm, we live out our respective faiths as the truth. Yes, we have lived with plurality, but not with pluralism. Whether we are Buddhist, Muslim or Confucian, we have a firm conviction that what we believe and live by is truth which leads to authentic humanity or eternal life, and that other paths would lead to perversion and suffering.

But all this has changed now. With the impact of globalization, pluralism is spreading like wild fire, as rapidly as it is in the West. While this undermines traditional faiths and presents great opportunities for the gospel, it has nevertheless become a real threat to our proclamation of truth.

Pluralism is an ideology that proclaims that truth is a cultural construction, valid only for the culture that constructs it, with no bearing on another culture or system of meaning. No truth can claim to be true for all. All truth is relative. The pluralist pushes the point further, from cultures to individuals. The individual is now presumed to be the ultimate ground of reality, the foundation on which meaning and values are created. The pluralist believes that individuals create their own logic and construct their own world. So there can be as many worlds as there are individuals, and each is merely a web of beliefs true only for the individual who weaves it. So despite all the rhetoric about dialogue, pluralism has rendered all dialogues unnecessary and meaningless.

As truth is fabricated, it can be refabricated at will. It is therefore tentative and fluid, with no lasting bearing on anything. In condemning all truths to be radically relative and tentative, pluralism can in effect silence any proclamation of transcendent eternal truth.

Pluralism frames anti-pluralist concepts of truth as dogmatic and exclusive, yet it is in essence the most dogmatic of all ideologies. Pluralism as such is the most virulent form of monism – it is the monism of indifference. However, it is not difficult to see the self-contradiction. In proclaiming pluralism, pluralists tacitly claim a vantage point, towering above everybody so as to see their relativity. Yet miraculously, the vantage point on which they stand is presumed to be absolute. How do they manage to do that? Purely by faith.

While trivializing truth and framing religious truth as oppressive, many pluralists nevertheless unashamedly promote the secular worldview to be true for all. Atheism is allowed to become the new religion, and is promoted as scientific, objective and inclusive. It is now waging a war against religion in general, and Christianity in particular, with unprecedented evangelistic zeal.

The 'Atheist Bus Campaign' in London is a good example. In June 2008, the campaign started with an advertisement on London buses saying, 'There is probably no God. Stop worrying. Enjoy your life.' The campaign has now spread to Canada. In a similar advertisement, two kids are posted, each pleading not to be labelled as a Catholic kid or an atheist kid – they want to be brought up neutral. In a very subtle way, the campaign condemns parents for raising their children with any conviction of truth. The monism of indifference is tightening its grip on our lives. Yet at the same time, books proclaiming atheism flood the market. Richard Dawkins' *The God Delusion* has been translated into thirty-one languages, with over 1.5 million copies sold to date.

> [Atheism] is now waging a war against religion in general, and Christianity in particular, with unprecedented evangelistic zeal.

Joan Bakewell, a columnist for *The Guardian*, sounded the battle-cry against religion in her praise of Dawkins' book: 'Religions have the secular world running scared. This book is a clarion call to cower no longer.'[2] What is the battle all about? It is about taking back the right to define moral values for oneself over against any transcendent boundary. Such a secular ideology has consequences, for the eclipse of transcendent truth has life implications.

Just months before the events in Tiananmen Square in Beijing on 4 June 1989, a well-known Chinese intellectual, Liu Xiaobo, wrote, 'The tragedy of the Chinese people is a tragedy of a people without God. When the light from the transcendent Other Side vanished, the darkness of this side will come to be taken as infinite light.'[3] A society without the transcendent light would almost certainly absolutize itself and turn even its own darkness into eternal light, sinking into the darkness of its own corruption.

Truth has consequences on the personal level as well. At the Amsterdam 2000 conference,[4] Dr Ravi Zacharias shared his experience of defending the objectivity of moral truth to a group of Oxford students. When he had finished, a student challenged him: 'Dr Ravi, morality is purely emotive. "Right" or "wrong" express nothing more than personal preference in an emotional way.' Ravi responded, 'If that were true, let us put it to the test. Let me put an innocent and helpless baby on the table and chop him up into three pieces with a big knife. Would you not say that what I have done is wrong?' Calmly the student answered, 'No, I would not say that; I can only say that I do not like it.' Ravi confessed that he was quite shocked.

Alas, if I had been there, I would have asked the student, 'What if I put *you* on this table, ready to chop you up into pieces, would you not say what I am going to do is wrong and ought to be stopped immediately?' And if he had said, 'All I can say is, I do not like it', then I would have said, 'I like it. I like it very much, and I happen to have the power to do it.'

Without the divine decree that human beings are created in the image of God (affirmed by God to have absolute value and to be absolutely inviolable), why should anyone take seriously the foundation of democracy that 'all are born equal'? Do we believe this because we like the idea? Or do we want to believe it rationally, out of self-interest, or perhaps fear? What if Nietzsche is right, that we invent such hollow statements, fearing that we are weak, and that only the strong and mighty will survive? 'Why should I believe that I was born equal to you, when I am genetically smarter and stronger than you? We are not born equal!' the smarter and the stronger would say. Should they have more votes in the political process?

If moral values were cut from their transcendent source, then the highest virtue could only be pragmatic function. In the context of a global market controlled by global corporations, the value of the human being lies in marketability or functionality, as a tool or a commodity. In such a world, people like Richard Posner would be right, when he says in his book, *Sex and Reason*,[5] that there is no real difference between prostitution and marriage. Marriage is basically long-term prostitution, an arrangement for the exchange of services between couples, whereas prostitution is a spot-market relationship; the payment made to the prostitute can then be used for purchasing services from others.

Right before our eyes, we see the moral fabric of our social life being torn to pieces, as humans are depersonalized and viewed as commodities or sets of functions:

> . . . for the world which seems
> To lie before us like a land of dreams,
> So various, so beautiful, so new,
> Hath really neither joy, nor love, nor light,
> Nor certitude, nor peace, nor help for pain;
> And we are here as on a darkling plain
> Swept with confused alarms of struggle and flight,
> Where ignorant armies clash by night.[6]

We are swept along by confusing ideologies, sinking deep into emptiness and alienation, consumed by unquenchable desires, with families broken up, societies fragmented and Mother Earth devastated.

To turn back the tide, we have to preach the gospel of Jesus Christ fearlessly, for he is the way, the truth and the life.

Only Jesus Christ can lead us away from the present state of godlessness, where the terror of man-made idols and selfish desires hold us captivated and perverted; where meaninglessness and silent despair seep into our bones. Jesus Christ, the way, leads us back to God the Creator, the source of meaning and goodness.

Jesus Christ is the truth because he is the foundation of all things. He is the Logos who sustains the universe, and in him the divine and the human come together in union. Truth reveals to us that the whole universe is created to manifest God's love.

Jesus Christ is the life, for he shows us life as it should be: life in communion with God, infused with purpose, with a sense of wholeness. True life knows the freedom to love and live life to the full, open to the infinite richness of God.

Truth cannot prove itself by anything other than itself. Jesus Christ did not prove himself by appealing to anything other than himself. He proved himself by his life of sacrificial love. Likewise, we can only prove to the world that Jesus Christ is the truth by his transforming power in our lives, something not even the pluralist can refute. Let us therefore preach Jesus Christ with our lives.

Carver Yu is President and Professor in Dogmatics at the China Graduate School of Theology, Hong Kong, and a member of the Lausanne Theology Working Group. www.cgst.edu

WHY WE NEED A HIGH VIEW OF TRUTH
Os Guinness (UK)

> There are times when history and the gospel of Jesus
> converge to create a dynamic thrust forward in human affairs.
> So it was with the 'gifts' of the gospel, such as philanthropy,
> the reform movements, the universities and modern science.
>
> There are other times when history and the gospel collide,
> and the titanic struggle shapes history in a different but
> equally decisive way. So it was when the lordship of Christ
> triumphed over the might of imperial Rome.
>
> There are still other times when history and the gospel
> *appear* to collide. But in fact the gospel speaks to the deepest
> dilemmas and the highest aspirations of the times that oppose
> it. So it is now with the gospel and the concept of truth.

At first sight, the biblical view of truth is obscene to modern minds
– 'arrogant', 'exclusive', 'intolerant', 'divisive' and 'judgmental'. But
taking a deeper look, it is profound, timely and urgent, even for
those who reject it. Regardless of what the wider world thinks, we
follow the One who declared that he is 'the way, *the truth* and the
life'. We therefore worship and serve the God of truth, whose Word
is truth, and who himself is true and to be trusted for his covenant
faithfulness.

I will give you six reasons why truth matters supremely to us, and
why Christians who are careless about truth are as wrong, as foolish
and as dangerous as the open sceptics and scoffers:

1. *Only a high view of truth honours the God of truth.* Too often,
    truth is considered merely a philosophical issue. For us,
    the philosophical issues are crucial and always to be taken
    seriously, but *truth is primarily a matter of theology.* Our Lord

God is actually, objectively, really and truly *there*, so what we believe by faith corresponds to the reality of *what is*. Our Lord is the true One, in the sense that he is the One whose covenant loyalty can be trusted, and the entire weight of our existence is staked on him. Those who weaken their hold on truth weaken their hold on God.

Truth is primarily a matter of theology.

2. *Only a high view of truth reflects how we come to know and trust God.* Jesus is the only way to God, though there are as many ways to Jesus as people who come to him. The record of the Scriptures and the experience of the centuries show there are three main reasons why we believe. We come to faith in Christ because (i) we are driven by our human needs; (ii) he seeks for us and finds us; and (iii) we are convinced that the claims of Christ and his gospel are *true*.

Because of truth, our faith in God is not irrational. It is not an emotional crutch. It is not a psychological projection or a matter of wish-fulfilment. It is not the opiate of the masses. Faith goes beyond reason because there is more to us as humans than our reason. Our faith is a warranted faith because we have come to the firm conviction that it is true. We are those who *think* in believing, and who *believe in thinking*.

3. *Only a high view of truth empowers our best human enterprises.* Sceptics and relativists who undermine the notion of truth are like fools who cut off the branch on which they are sitting. Without truth, (i) the great enterprise of science and all human knowledge collapse into conjecture; (ii) the vital profession of journalism and our ability to understand the events of the day and discern the signs of the times dissolve into rumour; (iii) the worlds of politics and business melt down into rules and power games; (iv) the precious gift of human freedom becomes license, and all human relations lose the element of trust that is their vital bonding. We are therefore unashamed to stand in the world as servants and

guardians of truth, both for God and for the highest
endeavours of humanity.

4. *Only a high view of truth can undergird our proclamation and defence
   of the faith.* If our Lord is the God of truth, we gladly affirm
   with the early church that 'All truth is God's truth.' We
   welcome and affirm all ideas, arguments and claims that
   pass the muster of God's standard of truth. But we also
   know that all humans, including we ourselves, are not only
   truth-seekers but *truth-twisters*. All unbelief 'holds the truth in
   unrighteousness'. We have the grounds as well as the duty
   to confront false ideas and false beliefs. We do this with the
   assurance that they are neither true, nor are they in the best
   interests of those who hold them – so we do people a
   service when we challenge them.

   Our stand for truth today must start in the church. We
   dare not shrink from this, as we remember how the apostle
   Paul challenged the apostle Peter. We must resist the siren
   seductions of those who downplay truth over against
   methodology, who confuse truth with activism, who
   exchange truth for entertainment, who mute truth for seeker-
   sensitivity, and who replace proclamation with conversation,
   or reduce solid substance to soundbites, and above all those
   who put a modern and revisionist view of truth in the place
   of the biblical view.

   Let there be no mistake. Whatever the motive, all such
   seductions lead to a weak and compromised faith, and end
   only in sorrow and yet another betrayal of our Lord. To
   abandon truth is to abandon faithfulness, and so to commit
   theological adultery and eventually spiritual suicide. Let the
   sorry fate of Protestant liberalism be a warning to us all.
   Down that way lies the final end of all 'kissing Judases' –
   those who betray Jesus yet again with a kiss and an unfaithful
   interpretation.

5. *Only a high view of truth is sufficient for resisting evil and hypocrisy.*
   Postmodern thinking makes us aware of hypocrisy as never

before, but gives us no standard of truth by which to expose and correct it. It calls us to 'authenticity', but offers us no truth to help attain it. With the global expansion of markets through capitalism, the global expansion of freedom through travel and technology, and the global expansion of human dysfunctions through the erosion of traditional ties and bonds, we face a perfect storm of globalized evil, including horrendous crimes such as human slavery and trafficking.

Hypocrisy and evil both depend on lies – hypocrisy being a lie in deeds rather than words, and evil always using lies to cover its oppressions. Only with truth can we stand up to deception and manipulation. Truth is the absolute necessity for all who hate hypocrisy, care for justice, defend human dignity and fight against evil.

6. *Only a high view of truth will help our growth and transformation in Christ.* Just as Abraham was called to 'walk before God', so we are called to follow 'the way of Jesus'. Our task is not just to *believe* the truth, or even to *know* and *defend* the truth. Our calling is so to *live in truth* that we are shaped by truth in our innermost beings, until by the grace of God we become people of truth.

Let there be no uncertainty about our commitment to truth, as followers of Christ. Shame on those Christians in the West who casually dismiss or scornfully deny what our Lord declared, what the Scriptures defend, and what our sisters and brothers die for rather than deny – that Jesus Christ our Lord is 'the way, the truth and the life'. Let us say, as the great German Reformer said of truth in regard to the Evil One, 'One little word will fell him.' Let us say with our sister, the American poet, 'Truth is my country.' Let us boldly declare with our brother, the Danish philosopher, 'Truth or nothing.' Let us demonstrate with our brother, the great Russian novelist and dissident, 'One word of truth outweighs the entire world.'

If our faith is not true, it would be false even if the whole world believed it. If our faith *is* true, it would be true even if the whole world and the entire cosmos were against it. So let the conviction ring out: we evangelicals do not just *believe* the truth. We do not just claim to *know* the truth and to *defend* it. We worship the God of truth, whose Spirit is the Spirit of truth, whose Word is truth, whose gospel is the message of truth, and whose Son our Lord is the way, the truth and the life.

May we ourselves be committed, humbly but resolutely, to becoming people of truth. Here we still stand, so help us God. As evangelicals, we are 'people of the good news'. May we also always be people of truth, worthy of the God of truth. God is true – so God is greater than all, and God can be trusted in all situations. Have faith in God! Have no fear! Hold fast to truth!

Os Guinness, author and social critic, and great-great grandson of the Dublin brewer, is Senior Fellow at the Oxford Centre for Christian Apologetics. www.theocca.org

TRUTH IN THE WORKPLACE:
EQUIPPING THE WHOLE CHURCH
Willy Kotiuga (Canada)

Workplace mission

The church teaches us to go into the whole world, but it has not equipped believers with tools and understanding of how God views the workplace. Yet how we view work influences the way we act at work. Do we see work as a necessary evil? Or do we perceive ways in which we can influence people through the work we do? For some, there is an immediate link, for example in the case of those working in public policy, or in product design, or as financial advisors, or in schools, or in academic administration or in the media. But all of us who serve, in whatever roles, can bring 'the aroma of Christ' to the way we engage with colleagues, competitors, clients and customers.

Christian believers are spread throughout all segments of the workplace. Some invite colleagues to join them on their faith journey. Others, while not talking about their personal faith with colleagues, allow it to shape their behaviour. The fields are ripe for harvest. In the workplace there are many potential harvesters, but only a small percentage are actually engaged in proclaiming hope to a world looking for hope.

> We are to rub in salt and shine light wherever our sphere of influence extends.

We are to rub in salt and shine light wherever our sphere of influence extends. This call is not only for church staff or those in Christian agencies, but for all of us in ordinary occupations. In this context, we could be called 'the church at large'.

The call to work came in Genesis 2, before the fall. It is good and worthy to work. Joseph's faith sustained him through four separate careers (family business, household management, prison

administration and public service). Indeed, it was key in his rise
to the top in each role. The apostle Paul used his skills as a tent-
maker to support his missionary endeavour, but also as a means of
reaching an audience who did not engage in public discussion on
faith-related matters. Daniel rose to the highest ranks, despite
personal risk to his life, because of his God-given wisdom and
unswerving commitment to God's principles. For each of them,
work was an offering of excellence to God.

Where are we now?

Paul's tentmaking inspired a generation to use their professional skills
as an entry point to cultures that were closed to 'formal' missionary
work. These 'tentmaking' professionals have worked hard as civil
servants, engineers, teachers and in many other professions. The
Business as Mission (BAM) movement has taken this one step further,
encouraging and equipping entrepreneurs to set up self-sustaining
businesses, which provide living examples of the Holy Spirit working
through people and demonstrate that honest practice works as the
best business model. Biblical wisdom is always practical wisdom.

Throughout the world, in small businesses and large corporations,
men and women of faith meet for Bible study and fellowship before
work or over lunch. These Bible studies, often open to colleagues
searching for truth, help build Christians up in their faith, and
provide a means for other workers to
find God. There are also nationwide
associations for Christians within professions, which stimulate a biblical
worldview, and help younger members,
often converted at university, to find other Christians in their
profession.

**Biblical wisdom
is always practical
wisdom.**

Christianity is a missionary faith, and the call to 'make disciples'
implores us to live out that faith by inviting others to join us on our
faith journey – and then by teaching them to obey everything Christ
has taught us. Sadly, the disconnect between Sunday and the working
week has left so many people with an 'incomplete' calling.

Where do we want to be?

Imagine a work environment with a vibrant relevant proclamation of faith, empowered by a moving of the Holy Spirit and supported by the invigorating prayers of the local church. Do we actually pray for our church members as they go into the new working week? Or do we pray only, or mostly, for church members who are in 'spiritual ministry'?

Rethinking 'how we do church' has become a catchphrase. Most efforts have been directed towards improving and refining existing programmes. But are there new questions to ask? I can think of remarkable stories of how God has been moving in churches willing to rethink how they live out the good news.

There is huge potential for church growth in the next generation in the form of those who hunger for meaningful relationships in the workplace. Increasingly, multi-ethnic work environments in the West offer opportunity to enter into the lives of people from all nations.

We need to think more deeply about how to equip workers to live and proclaim their faith, rather than just to *be* a Christian presence at work. Properly equipped, and with a holistic God-view of the workplace, these people could be highly motivated harvesters. But first, the church needs to recognize God's call into the secular professions as being a real call, as real as the call into spiritual ministry. 'The earth is the Lord's', and we need to reclaim it for him in industry, academia, medicine and the public arena.

How do we get there?

There is no universal recipe, but there can be key steps to moving closer to what God intends for us.

For years now, the church and the secular have been kept in separate spheres. In church we learn more of the good news and how God wants to bring hope to the world. But on Monday, week after week, we offer no invitation to co-workers to discover God's grace, forgiveness and hope. So the gap between theology and praxis grows, and church becomes increasingly irrelevant to the workplace, while the workplace becomes irrelevant to the church.

Workers and pastors live in different paradigms. Many pastors have spent their careers in professional ministry and don't fully understand work dynamics. And workers have not attempted to educate pastors on the workplace. As a result, they stay in their respective worlds, meeting only at church functions. When a worker has taken his pastor on a tour of the workplace, this has often proved very enriching for the pastor and for his ministry.

Two things need to happen if the church–work divide is to be bridged: rethinking the role of the church in supporting our workplace emissaries, and rethinking the role of work in motivating emissaries.

Christian influence can bring radical change, through the modelling of honest practice at every level, as well as through the influence of Christian thinking at a senior level. Our workplace needs to be seen as an opportunity to contribute Christian thinking and also bring God's love to people.

The Business as Mission (BAM) movement has demonstrated that we need to be more intentional about penetrating the workplace. Its focus on the practical aspect of equipping Christian entrepreneurs to succeed should become part of church culture. Sir Fred Catherwood opens this out with practical advice and inspiration in his short, persuasive *Light, Salt and the World of Business*.[7] He argues that the public arenas are interdependent, and that each is rooted in the influence of the universities. He then shows how good practice can change values in nations. It takes courage and passion to invest one's life in the BAM movement, and it takes a willingness to put everything at risk.

We have good motivational books, studies and examples – and enough guilt about not doing enough – to make a good start. What we don't have is the critical mass to build and create momentum to make the process sustainable.

Everything that we do is a gift to God, whether it be preaching, teaching, designing, cooking, cleaning, creating spreadsheets or operating machines. All work has dignity, and all our work should reflect excellence that is a worthy offering acceptable to God.[8] We must educate church members on how to see work as their calling from God, and help clergy to see the mission possibilities in the workplace.

The Joseph Model

Moving from where we are to where we want to be will not happen overnight. There is no magic formula or instruction manual to guarantee results.

God has blessed me with a sacred workplace where I serve him as a professional consulting engineer. I call it the 'Joseph Model', in honour of Joseph who transformed each of his work environments, under adverse conditions.

We need to be committed to ongoing transformation through a daily walk with God. As we plant gospel seeds, there will be many variables outside our control, impeding growth. After years of trying to invite co-workers to join me on a faith journey, I realized that words and a personal example were not enough. Now I start the discipling process from the moment someone comes into my sphere of influence. I have the privilege of being a director in the company. This means I have a responsibility to create an environment which is conducive to creating an excellent product and helping people attain their highest potential.

I lead a skilled group of professional engineers with projects in over twenty countries. Our primary output is high-level consulting reports for governments, international funding agencies and senior electricity company executives. The values driving our work environment include accountability, responsibility, the pursuit of excellence, teamwork, discussion in a learning environment, risk-taking, forgiveness, support and celebration. These values, desirable professionally, help people embark on a faith journey and are an integral part of making good disciples. Let's look at them:

> *Accountability* reinforces that in all areas of life we are accountable to a higher authority.
> *Responsibility* reinforces that we should work through difficulties to meet obligations and commitments.

The pursuit of excellence motivates people to do better than they have done in the past, and better than others are used to doing. *Teamwork* means mutual respect for one another's gifts, and a desire to work towards a goal rather than for one's own aggrandizement.

A learning environment stimulates discussion and encourages exploration to discover more about life.

Risk-taking helps staff learn to step out of their comfort zone.

Forgiveness is offered to those who make mistakes, or whose risks have not turned out to be successful.

Support enables people to move in confidence to the next level of understanding and knowledge.

Celebration is appropriate for the whole team as we share in one another's successes.

These are all Christian values relating to the life of faith. Such an ambience provides for professional excellence and for co-workers to be discipled long before they make a commitment to faith. So when they meet Jesus and cross into a life of faith, they enter a lifestyle that is already somewhat familiar.

This is the sacred environment in which I live at my workplace. For others not in managerial positions, the holy ground may be limited to one's shared workspace, desk or workbench. For some, a sacred workplace is the lunchtime Bible study once a week. For others, it could be coffee breaks and/or lunchtimes filled with discussions (not monologues) about life issues. Ultimately, what transforms the secular to sacred is the presence of God – and when God is present, changes take place. We are all called to be change agents. If Joseph could do it as a slave and as a prisoner, there is no reason why we cannot transform *our* sphere of influence into holy ground.

The future is full of possibilities for reaching billions of workers around the world. Let's endeavour to energize, train and equip church members to practise their faith, at whatever level they serve, and to make an impact for the gospel – on the assembly line or at the head of a corporation. Let's explore ways to help workers develop leadership skills, as Christians, confident that all biblical wisdom is practical wisdom.

May God open our eyes and break down the barriers we have created so that we can prepare the workplace for a faith journey.[9]

Willy Kotiuga is Senior Director of the Power Systems Consulting Group in one of the world's largest engineering firms.

www.businessasmissionnetwork.com www.licc.org.uk

SHARING THE IRRESISTIBLE
TRUE CHRIST
Rebecca Manley Pippert (USA)

The gospel is good news, the most glorious news ever to grace our weary and battered planet. Yet so many Christians feel inadequate when it comes to sharing their faith. Why does the church often struggle in training believers to share the glorious gospel with confidence?

Following years of evangelism training and outreach, I am more convinced than ever that we must develop a (i) biblically based, (ii) theologically sound, (iii) culturally relevant and (iv) relationally effective approach, if we are to be effective in bearing witness to Christ. Our emphasis must not be on numbers or techniques, but on authenticity, credibility and spiritual power. Enabling the church to know Christ well – and to make him well known – that is our *global* challenge.

The issues we face in communicating 'the best news ever' are wide and deep. In the past ten years, my husband and I have conducted evangelism training conferences and evangelistic outreaches in the Global South (Africa, Latin America and Asia) and the Global North (Europe, Australia and N. America). At present we are living and ministering primarily in Europe, perhaps the most difficult place in the world in which to talk about the good news. What issues must we address if we are to develop a holistic understanding of evangelism?

Our theology must impact on our methodology
There has been a tendency in the West (which has been copied by others) to focus evangelism training simply on learning techniques. But techniques do not motivate us at a deeper level, nor are they effective in building authentic relationships. This isn't to diminish the importance of offering practical help. But the practical must be framed within a deeper theological understanding. Our effectiveness

in witness does not come from learning new *methods*, but from understanding the *message*. Our freedom to witness comes from understanding the author of the message: God himself! In other words, *our theology must impact on our methodology.* Understanding the character of God will be the deepest possible motivation for witness.

A three-pronged response to evangelism in the global era

The strongest and most vital evangelism occurs when three approaches are used together: *personal evangelism, small-group evangelism* and *proclamation evangelistic events.* These three approaches complement one another. When we use all three together, the result is powerful! So as a church, we must provide solid training in personal and small-group witness, *and* put on creative and contextually sensitive outreach events. Let's look at what is needed to support public proclamation, under two headings.

1. Personal evangelism

Most Christians feel inadequate when it comes to being a witness for Christ. They fear saying or doing the wrong thing. In every culture we find people raising the same issues, especially as they relate to personal witness: *What if we offend? What if they ask us questions we can't answer? How do we bring up the topic of faith naturally? How can we be a witness when our own lives are so imperfect? How do we share the gospel in ways that are culturally relevant, biblically faithful and contextually sensitive?*

Our model for evangelism is the incarnation of Christ.

Has Christ given us a model for how to engage in evangelism? He has! Christ gave us a model, a message and the means, both to incarnate and proclaim the good news of God's transforming love in our broken world.

The model: embody the story

Our model for evangelism is the incarnation of Christ, a theological lens through which we view our entire missional task. Our inspiration, motivation and practice must come from understanding the unique act in history where God entered into our world and our human condition, in the person of Jesus Christ.

Jesus said, 'As the Father sent me, so I am sending you' (John 20:21). Jesus is telling us that our mission in the world is to resemble his. Just as he entered our world, so are we to enter others' worlds.

Jesus said that the essence of the law is to 'love the Lord your God with all your heart and with all your soul and with all your strength and . . . your neighbour as yourself' (Luke 10:27). The Trinity, the law and the ministry of Jesus all point to the same truth: *the kingdom of God is profoundly relational.* When we reach out and express God's love to others, we are reflecting the deepest reality of all: the very triune nature of God. Jesus loved the sinful, the lost, the maimed, the marginalized – and so must we.

But how do we demonstrate God's love to seekers without compromising our own identity? The incarnation of Jesus is the supreme example of identification without the loss of identity. People in Jesus' day thought holy men could be found only in synagogues, but Jesus went to the market place. He had a 'go-to-them' rather than a 'come-to-us' approach. But Jesus remained in the Father: he knew who he was, and therefore was not at risk of giving in to the culture around him. Likewise, Jesus invites us to remain in him and promises to remain in us if we do (John 15:4).

The kingdom of God is profoundly relational.

I recently asked a student at Queen's University in Belfast, Northern Ireland, if she was developing authentic and genuine friendships with seekers. She responded, 'Oh, my church wouldn't approve of me socializing with unbelievers. The marching order from my minister before I left for university was, "Just come back to us a Christian!"'

I feel sympathy for this pastor. I understand his fear that, by living in a culture that is increasingly hostile to faith, this student might be swept away and her witness compromised. Yet how can we be Christ's agents to a hurting world if all we offer is a 'fortress' mentality where the only goal is preservation? Jesus didn't call us to a 'holy huddle' but to be 'light' and 'salt'.

The message: tell the story

Expressing the love of Christ in the context of relationship is foundational to witness, but establishing loving friendships isn't all that God requires of us. God also asks us to bear witness to the truth. That means we must also tell the story. But therein lies the crunch, especially in the West. How do we bravely, faithfully and creatively proclaim the gospel in our age of relativism that denies the possibility of truth in any absolute sense? When the truth of any truth is under suspicion and the validity of gospel truth is either denied, ignored or considered arrogant? Yet we are told these unflinching, foundational truths: 'By this gospel you are saved . . . that Christ died for our sins according to the Scriptures, that he was buried, that he was raised on the third day according to the Scriptures, and that he appeared' (1 Corinthians 15:2–5).

If we are not faithful to the gospel, then the work of evangelism will never be effective. But when Christians feel intimidated about telling others the Christian message, it is not just a fear of rejection. It goes deeper, to the ability to *believe the message themselves* in a world that tells them that a religious conviction cannot be true in any factual sense and must be held only as a private opinion. Our task is therefore to strengthen the modern believer's confidence that this 'good news' is not just true *for them*, but true for the whole world, and can be told with assurance.

The means: feed on the Spirit

Besides declaring God's truth, we must also depend on the power of the Holy Spirit. Our lack of dependence on the Spirit's power is perhaps the single most glaring deficiency in the modern Western church compared with the early church or churches in the Global South. If we are going to be witnesses in the twenty-first century, it is critical that we have the power of the Spirit residing in us, flowing through us, bringing the character of Jesus into us. We must rediscover that prayer is a holy weapon to be used in evangelism and in our spiritual battles. We must ask God to empower us with the gifts of the Spirit. It is after all the Spirit of God that produces transformed lives, not our ability to communicate the gospel perfectly.

2. Small-group evangelism

One method that we've found very effective in evangelism is this: once friendships with seekers are established and there is freedom in discussing spiritual issues, consider inviting them to a seeker Bible study. This is a question-based study in which the majority of people who come are seekers or sceptics, not Christians. We invite them to come to a neutral place (our home, our school dorm, the back of a restaurant) to look at one of the Gospels and examine the life of Jesus. We tell them they don't have to believe in God or believe that the Bible is the Word of God. We simply invite them to 'come and see'.

Seeker study is effective because it isn't a slick programme or a gimmick, but is based on relationships. It is dialogical, not didactic. Truth is presented through story, not a sermon. It is process-oriented and fosters authentic relationships. We're not inviting strangers, but friends. People who wouldn't darken the door of a church feel comfortable coming to our home where they are with people like themselves – people with lots of unanswered questions. We provide a safe place for those who may never have read the Bible or whose understanding of Christianity is at best sketchy. And while some may have been turned off by religious organizations like the church, many are still curious about Jesus: *Who was he? What was he like? What did he say and do?* I believe the greatest shortcut to evangelism is focusing on the person of Jesus, because Jesus is irresistible! I have seen even the most cynical feel drawn to Jesus, whether or not they eventually become Christ-followers, which bodes well for future discussions.

> **Seeker study is dialogical, not didactic.**

We have seen seeker studies started in every country where we have ministered. At this moment there are literally hundreds of seeker studies taking place in the UK among university students, with reports of conversions coming in regularly.

After one of our Salt Shaker Conferences in a country where people cannot openly practise Christianity, a woman wrote that she was leading a seeker study for her professional colleagues, which was quite risky:

> The people came because they trusted me. We were already friends, and they'd become curious about my faith. These are people who had never read one word of the Bible and knew almost nothing about Jesus. But they quickly became engaged, and their curiosity was aroused as we read the passages each week. But what fascinated me most was how Jesus became alive to them. They commented on their surprise in seeing how relevant these Bible stories were to their own lives. Several in the group have now given their lives to Christ.

A microbiologist in Italy invited her research colleagues to come to her apartment for pasta and a study on 'Who is the real Jesus?' Most of them were atheists and, as fellow research scientists, had had countless conversations on science versus faith, the New Atheism, evolution and so forth. What drew them to come was their respect for her, her obvious love for them, the fact that she took their questions seriously, and her irrepressible joy. She recently wrote to us again to say that the most vociferous atheist of the group had just committed his life to Christ.

'To be always relevant, you have to say things which are eternal.'

How could reading Bible stories about Jesus who lived 2,000 years ago possibly seem relevant to modern people from cultures so vastly different? The late French philosopher Simone Weil was on to something when she wrote, 'To be always relevant, you have to say things which are eternal.' In other words, true spiritual power lies in utilizing God's eternal resources: his Word (the living Word and the written Word) and his Spirit. A seeker study is effective because it is centred on authentic relationship, while at the same time utilizing the power of God's Word and Spirit – which makes it eternally relevant!

One of my fears is that the world looks at Christians from a distance and concludes that Jesus' primary task is to help us have devotions and to keep us from swearing. But when they encounter the biblical Jesus, they realize this Jesus would never flee from someone struggling with a sexual addiction, substance abuse or an eating disorder. He doesn't walk away from brokenness. He is willing to wade into our mess and love us where we are. Most people can't imagine a God who is willing to become deeply involved in our messy lives. But that is our task – to emulate Christ, to show them who he is, and to share how he has mended our own brokenness and forgiven our sins.

Let us remember that evangelism is a life before it is a task. We are on dangerous ground when we allow techniques to take precedence over theology, when human strategy replaces trust in God's Word, and when we rely on programmes instead of the power of the Holy Spirit. We have been given an infinitely credible gospel, so let us be credible messengers who demonstrate not clever methodology, but authenticity, integrity and spiritual power.

Evangelism is a life before it is a task.

If the world is to be evangelized in this century, if by God's mercy we are to see revival, it will take genuine repentance within the church, divine cleansing, holy living and fresh empowerment by the Holy Spirit. What we need is a renewed vision of who Christ is, and what he has come to do: heal, restore and transform all of life! If we live out this vision as true disciples, evangelism cannot help but happen.

Rebecca Manley Pippert is an author, evangelist and a widely used speaker. She is the founder of Salt Shaker Ministries. www.saltshaker.org

DAY 2

RECONCILIATION: Building the peace of Christ in our divided and broken world

TESTIMONY: PALESTINIAN–JEWISH RECONCILIATION
Shadia Qubti and Dan Sered

Shadia: 'There is room only for us in this land, if we are to be free.'

This is what my world teaches. But 2 million Palestinians, including myself, challenge this divide because we are a part of the Palestinian people, yet we hold Israeli citizenship. Ten per cent of us are Christian among a majority of Muslim Palestinians. We are a minority among a minority, struggling in a world calling for exclusion.

It was in my first Musalaha that I met with Israeli Messianic believers. I felt uncomfortable and threatened. I had grown up in a Baptist church in Nazareth where I had accepted Jesus as my Saviour. But it was in that encounter with Israeli Messianic believers that I truly understood that through Christ I was reconciled to God, and as a follower of Christ I had a responsibility to be reconciled with my enemies. Without this reconciliation, Jesus' act on the cross is not complete.

As a Palestinian, it's very difficult to reach out to my enemies. But as a Christian Palestinian, I can do so. Because Jesus gives me the eyes to see them as he sees me. Jesus gives me the confidence to go against my society. He gives me the power to embrace them. Today when I meet Israeli Messianic believers, I feel close, I feel comfortable, and most importantly, I feel at home. I have decided *to dedicate my life to Musalaha, to pursue and promote reconciliation between Israelis and Palestinians. In the Messiah there is room for all of us; he calls us to be one family. Reconciliation has changed me. Reconciliation changes my enemy, and only through reconciliation can we become the greatest witness, the living stones; only then can it change those around us.*

Dan: *My mother is not proud of me being a believer in Jesus, and my father would be outraged if he knew that I was standing here next to a Palestinian. You see, I'm a good Jewish boy who was raised in Israel in a typical secular home. My father had a long career in the Israeli military, and his job with the Ministry of Defence uprooted our family to New York. I was only fourteen when we moved. Unlike my parents, even at a young age I believed in the existence of God. At Stony Brook University while studying maths, I met a Jewish girl named Dina who told me that Jesus' Hebrew name is Yeshua, 'salvation'. Dina showed me in the New Testament that Jesus has fulfilled all of the prophecies about the Messiah. My eyes were opened, and for the first time in my life being Jewish made sense to me.*

This was the beginning of reconciliation in my life. Immediately I felt a burden to share this news with my Jewish people so that they too could be reconciled to God. Now I serve with Jews for Jesus. We exist to make the Messiahship of Jesus an unavoidable issue for Jewish people worldwide. We want to see the gospel going back to the Jewish people.

Talking about my Jewish people, the apostle Paul said, 'For if their rejection is the reconciliation of the world, what will their acceptance be but life from the dead?' (Romans 11:15, NIV). You see, the rejection of the Jewish nation of Messiah brought about reconciliation to the world. Aren't you glad about that?

Today, living in the land of Israel, an unreached nation, hostile to the gospel, makes me realize the reconciling power of the gospel. When Israeli Jews and Palestinian Arabs can say to one another, 'I love you in Jesus' name', the world will see the powerful reconciling work of the good news. The only hope for peace for the Middle East is truly Jesus. Let's pray for the peace of Jerusalem and salvation for all the people of Israel.

Shadia Qubti serves with Musalaha in Galilee, an initiative for reconciliation between Christian Palestinians and Messianic Jews. Dan Sered directs Jews for Jesus in Israel. www.musalaha.org www.jewsforjesus.org

EPHESIANS 2
Ruth Padilla DeBorst (Argentina/Costa Rica)

Heaven truly is the place of God's dwelling. Heavenly places, we read in Ephesians 1, are the glorious seat of Christ's powerful rule. We celebrate as sons and daughters of the King who reigns from heaven on high, far above all rule and authority and power and dominion (1:21). Ephesians 2 invites us to consider how that cosmic reign is made visible in daily, tangible, breathing, human life. It helps us answer the question: Where does God live?

The apostle Paul is writing from prison to fellow-followers of Jesus in the port city of Ephesus and in the broader Asia Minor region. Through time – by conquest, colonization and emigration – Greeks, Persians, Romans and Jews had been added to the indigenous inhabitants of Anatolia. Diverse cultural, linguistic, socio-economic and religious expressions mixed and clashed, forced together by the hegemony (of Rome).

Traditions were being challenged and identities were shifting; many felt uprooted, at a loss – especially the people at the bottom of the totem pole. Officially, peace ruled. Borders were secured by the emperor's legions. Taxes and tributes may have felt burdensome – especially when the benefit was mostly seen in far-off centres of power – but they guaranteed security, stronger armies and taller walls. The slightest disturbance was swiftly repressed; torture was a common practice, and served as a deterrent. Temples were places of worship where conquering forces imposed their gods on the people incorporated into their domain.

Honour and unquestionable allegiance naturally were due to the emperor, the self-styled lord and saviour, who so effectively imposed peace and kept unity among such a multicultural, multi-ethnic and multi-religious array of people. Those were the days of the *Pax Romana.*

It is into this scene that Paul's words are read to the growing community of Christ-followers, some of Jewish descent like him, most of them Gentiles: 'You were dead in the trespasses and sins in which you once walked, following the course of this world, following the prince of the power of the air, the spirit that is now at work in the sons of disobedience.' They were lifeless, dragged along with no say by powers beyond their control; an existence of barren striving for personal success and satisfaction, directionless, like a sailboat with no rudder.

Paul has pretty strong words for the Gentiles. 'Ah, this is about *them*!' the Jewish Christians might have sighed in relief. 'This is not about *us*, the chosen Israel!' They could have been proud of their lineage and heritage (as direct descendants of God's people of old), and proud of their imperial culture, marked by 'might makes right'. They could have rested assured in their own sense of belonging; they could have believed *they* owned the right to determine who was *in* and who was *out* of the new community being forged by the apostles' teaching.

'Become like us, the true believers; look at the world through our lenses and organize your experience into our categories. Otherwise, you'll only ever be second-class. We can tolerate a little colour here and there, a token representative of minority groups. But they must be willing to blend in, to accommodate our standards and expectations, our jargon, our styles.' Yet Paul leaves no room for such self-righteousness. He continues: 'We all once lived in the passions of our flesh, carrying out the desires of the body and the mind, and were by nature children of wrath, like the rest of humankind' (verse 3). Jews and Gentiles alike: *all* were one in death, bound together by its eternal grip.

Reconciliation with God

'But God . . . ' continues Paul. (This is the turning point.) 'God, being rich in mercy, because of the great love with which he loved us' (verse 4) breaks into this hopeless picture. The one who initially breathed life into every living creature would not abandon the work of his hands. In the beginning, out of nothing, God had created and celebrated life as good; so again the Community-of-love

– Father, Son and Holy Spirit – steps into the deathly scene to grant full life, value and purpose to God's creatures.

Paul builds his case in crescendo. *First*, in Christ, God recreates humankind: 'Even when we were all dead in our trespasses, [God] made us alive together with Christ' (verse 5). This is good news for those first-century Christians, and also for us: 'Even when we were all dead in our trespasses, God made us alive together with Christ.' Thanks be to God!

Next, in Christ, God reinstates humankind: 'God . . . raised us up with him and seated us with him in the heavenly places in Christ Jesus.' Believe it or not, Paul reminds the weary, displaced people, you are now above it all, with Christ, in the heavenly places! You have been carried from dust to glory through no effort of your own. This is a fact! Yes, perhaps in the Roman Empire you are viewed as an insignificant handful of Christ-followers, under increasing suspicion for contesting the emperor's authority, and barely acknowledged as a tiny cog in the imperial machinery for the taxes you pay. However, in God's gracious economy, you are not dispensable, but rather valuable and beautiful. God fashions the community of Christ-followers together into a poem, his work of art, his masterpiece. Value and beauty are granted by our Creator to the Christian community, not fabricated by the symbols of status, prestige or prosperity of our contemporary, pagan consumer society.

Peace that rebuilds
God in Christ recreates and reinstates humankind as the expression of God's image in God's world. So finally, as he did in the beginning, God again grants humankind purpose: 'We . . . are created in Christ Jesus *for* good works, which God prepared beforehand, that we should walk in them' (verse 10). The creation mandates of family and work, responsible relationships and responsible productivity are restored in Christ. Our reign with Christ in heavenly places is to be given concrete, historical expression in our ethical behaviour here and now. Good works are a mark of new life and faithful discipleship; their absence, an indication of their lack.

Paul knows the imprisoning effect of pride and the dead-end street of self-righteous works. Years earlier, as a radical defender of the Jewish faith, he had gone on murderous rampages piously to eradicate what he considered a pernicious sect. But Jesus tore off his blinders, and the Spirit reoriented his will. Paul then saw that such striving did not bring him any closer to God. Only Christ did. 'But God . . . ' We cannot *earn* new life, new status or new purpose. It is God who grants them to us, 'so that in the coming ages he might show the immeasurable riches of his grace in kindness towards us in Christ Jesus [his undeserved favour]'. 'For by grace you have been saved through faith. And this is not your own doing.' Paul reminds his readers, 'It is the gift of God, not a result of works, so that no one may boast.' This we too must remember today.

The discipline of remembering provides the antidote to blinding, boastful pride:

> Remember that at one time you Gentiles in the flesh, called 'the uncircumcision' [classed as *out*siders] by what is called the circumcision [those who consider themselves *in*siders], which is made in the flesh by hands – remember that you were at that time separated from Christ, alienated from the commonwealth of Israel and strangers to the covenants of promise, having no hope and without God in the world.
>
> (verses 11–12)

Remember that once you were dead; we all were alienated from God, from one another, from the rest of creation. But that was before, back then.

Reconciliation that draws us towards peace

Paul dedicates verses 13–22 to describing the current picture, introducing the section with the words 'But now' to establish the striking contrast brought about by the gracious intervention of the Triune God: 'But now in Christ Jesus you who once were far off have been brought near by the blood of Christ. For he himself is our peace, who has made us both one and has broken down in his flesh the dividing wall of hostility.'

Pax Romana was fragile, pounded precariously together with cross nails and oppressive taxation. But one night, angels shattered the repressed silence with joyful songs of 'peace on earth'! They announced a different kind of peace to a weary people: the long-awaited Prince of Peace had broken into history in the shape of a poor, working-class baby in an insignificant corner, far from the seats of Roman and temple power. In his public ministry, Jesus' rule was not marked by military nor economic might. Instead, he gave himself away, granting sight to the blind, feeding the hungry, liberating the oppressed, and affirming the dignity of women, children and others who were marginalized in Jewish society. Rather than imposing security by repression and death, Jesus took on the scornful cross in loving sacrifice. In so doing, he unveiled as deceitful the powers of death that held humanity estranged from God, from one another and from the rest of creation. Christ, our peace, effected salvation, giving new life to the dead. He offered reconciled relations with God, healing from enmity to a broken humanity, restoration to the entire created order. This is surely good news of true peace: *Pax Christi*. Jesus *is* our peace.

Christ's peace and justice

Jesus also *makes* peace. During his life – 'in his flesh' – Jesus made peace by doing justice, by restoring to their rightful place and right relations those who were being deprived by unjust systems, human greed and an abuse of power. He put down the self-righteous religious leader and praised the socially despised tax collector. He healed lepers, the HIV-Aids victims of his day, and restored them to the community. He spoke with women, and called men to account regarding their treatment of them. He urged the wealthy to see the economic implications of discipleship. He lived out the historic script of God's prophets through the ages. Jesus made peace also through his death – 'through his blood'. When he died, the temple curtain separating off the Holy of Holies was ripped in half: now access to God was no longer restricted to certain people or times!

But the wonder does not end there: the risen Christ sends his disciples to the ends of the earth, far beyond the ethnic confines of Israel. Through the power of the Holy Spirit, they communicate the good news in many Gentile languages, and relate to 'unlikely' people – foreigners, women, pagan governors. The Spirit enables them to confront and eradicate exclusive laws and practices that do not allow the full participation of all disciples in the life and ministry of the Christian community.

Paul, the previously zealous Jew, began to live out his vocation as Christ's apostle to the Gentiles. As he wrote this letter, he was enduring prison for taking non-Jews into the temple, beyond the wall built to keep the *ins* in and the *outs* out! His conviction of God's cosmic reconciling purposes in Christ propelled Paul into his life mission: sacrificial efforts to breed unity, peace and justice within the new community.

Reconciliation to create relationship

So when both legalistic interpretations of Jewish law and Roman decrees prescribed oppressive relational patterns for women, children and slaves in family and at work, Paul daringly preached mutual submission to all, particularly to the powerful – men, fathers, employers – and he acknowledged the anointed roles of women, young people and non-Jewish Christians in the early church community. Paul lived by what he taught: Christ has 'abolished the law of commandments and ordinances, that he might create in himself one new man [a new humanity] in place of the two, so making peace, and might reconcile us both to God in one body through the cross, thereby killing the hostility' (verses 15–16). Thanks to Christ's peace-making life, death and ongoing ministry through the Spirit, Jesus-followers are now one, not in death but in Christ.

Paul daringly preached mutual submission to all.

Peace preaching

Finally, in Paul's words, Jesus 'came and *preached* peace'. 'He . . . preached peace to you who were far off and peace to those who were near. For through him we both have access in one Spirit to the Father.' Rhetoric, preaching, speaking, all these are skills practised and esteemed in the Greco-Roman society to which the recipients of Paul's letter belong. The hearers are highly aware of the power of the spoken word in building personal prestige and swaying public opinion. But Jesus' peace *preaching* had a far more significant impact: it was grounded in his peace *being* and his peace *making* as expressions of the ongoing reconciling work of the God who declares things into being. In the beginning, God, the creative Community-of-love, spoke the world into existence out of chaos. In Jesus, the Word made flesh, God spoke redemption and new life into history. And through the Spirit's breath, God speaks community out of distanced individuals. God speaks and it comes to pass.

Reconciliation for family/church membership

Paul had begun his letter portraying the grand cosmic scheme of things: everything brought together under Christ's lordship. He now zooms in to the visible, historical expression of that unity and authority. He leads us not to some ancient temple or opulent modern church building. Instead, he lands squarely on his listeners, the local community of Christ-followers: 'You are no longer strangers and aliens, but you are fellow citizens with the saints and members of the household of God' (verse 19). What God in Christ has spoken into being is nothing more and nothing less than the church, the body of Jesus' followers, the new humanity woven together out of people from different ethnic, linguistic, cultural and religious strands. Citizenship in the Roman Empire depended on lineage, power and financial means. Belonging in Jewish cultural religion rested on family line and social status. But membership in the household of God, by contrast, is a gift: Gentile and Jew, slave and free, women and men, old and young, people from South and North, East and

West, people without all their limbs or wits, and people with all their limbs and wits. All can belong.

This new household, the church, is built not on money or power, or the charisma of leaders, or individual saints, but on the foundation of the apostles and prophets, on the whole recorded history of God's work in God's world through all God's people. Rome claimed that imperial power holds everything together, and temples became symbols of dominion. Today we may be tempted to place confidence in nations, military or economic power, big church budgets or successful business ventures. We can become preoccupied with denominations or institutions, more so than with people. But with Paul, we must claim that the entire construction would crumble without Jesus Christ himself, 'the cornerstone, in whom the whole structure, being joined together, grows into a holy temple in the Lord' (verses 20–21).

What about us?

Where, we asked at the beginning, does God live? Paul closes with this amazing and humbling affirmation: 'In him [Christ] you also are being built together into a dwelling place for God by the Spirit' (verse 22). We, the church, with all our imperfections, petty concerns, pride and prejudice are God's holy temple, God's earthly home! Yes. By grace it is here, in this immensely diverse, trans-national, trans-ethnic, trans-cultural community that God chooses to live.

God lives in the new humanity created by God, reconciled by Christ, indwelt and diversely gifted by the Holy Spirit, for the building up of that community and for works of peace and justice far outside its bounds. God lives wherever men and women together allow the Community-of-love to imprint God's image on them, and to speak reconciliation in their midst. Unity becomes visible, reminding us that once we were *all* together in death and that our lives, our value and our purpose depend entirely on God's unmerited grace. God yearns to build the world church today into his earthly dwelling place!

Do we, each one of us, see ourselves as living stones that *must* fit together with others to compose God's living place? The most powerful testimony of God's love to the world is our reconciled relations, regardless of our nationality, ethnicity, political persuasion or financial status. When our families, neighbours, colleagues and communities look at our local congregation, are they struck by the loving and just relationships? Will we live out our calling to follow Jesus in his reconciling mission by being, making and boldly preaching peace? Will we allow God to write a new poem out of his world church today?

May we see ourselves as fruits and agents of *Pax Christi*, brought together by God's reconciling will in Christ and sent back into the world by the power of God's Spirit to incarnate God's good purposes for the entire cosmos. Let us tear down the walls of self-defence, security and prosperity that our greed, pride and prejudice have built, and become welcoming communities – even to people who are different from us. Let us pledge allegiance not to the Caesars of the day, but to the Lord of history, the only Prince of Peace. Let us celebrate today – in profound and repentant awe and grateful commitment – that we *are* God's dwelling place.

> Let us pledge allegiance to the Lord of history, the only Prince of Peace.

Ruth Padilla DeBorst, General Secretary of the Latin American Theological Fellowship, directs Ediciones Certeza Unida, an evangelical publishing house, and leads the Institute for the Promotion of Christian Higher Education in Latin America. www.ftl-al.org

OUR GOSPEL OF RECONCILIATION
Antoine Rutayisire (Rwanda)

I come to you as a Christian and a preacher, and also as a member of the National Unity and Reconciliation Commission established in the aftermath of the Rwanda genocide of 1994. I come from a wounded nation, a broken nation that is healing. I grew up wounded, angry, full of hatred and bitterness. But the cross of Jesus Christ has changed my life.

Flourishing churches and festering wounds

The fastest-growing churches are now in Africa, South America and South East Asia: regions that have witnessed wars, ethnic clashes, even genocides. How do we reconcile the joy of fast-growing churches with this history? Most countries with a dominant Christian presence in Africa are deeply wounded. If they look normal and healthy, then the healing is only superficial, with wounds underneath festering like a volcano ready to explode. We are not healed.

How can we be Christians and still live with hatred and anger? How can we live with slavery, apartheid, ethnic and racial hatred, family dislocation and divorce? What has gone wrong with our evangelization and Christian discipleship? What can we do to become 'ambassadors of reconciliation'? My plea is for a rediscovery of 'the gospel of reconciliation'.

Failure and success: Rwanda as a case study

The census of 1991 showed Rwanda as 89% Christian, with Roman Catholics (62%), Protestants (27%), and the rest of the population composed of traditionalists (8%), Muslims (1.5%), other religions (0.5%). The White Fathers, the first Catholic missionaries to arrive in Rwanda in 1901, came to create 'a Christian Kingdom in the heart of Africa', a dream long cherished by their founder, Cardinal Lavigerie. In 1941 the king of Rwanda was baptized. Chiefs and influential personalities followed suit, making Rwanda the epitome of a fulfilled dream. Protestant missionaries were also successful, despite merciless opposition by the Catholic missionaries who had carved out a lion's share for themselves. In the early 1930s, a mighty revival broke out in the Anglican Mission of Gahini, setting East Africa on fire. Uganda, Tanzania, Kenya, Burundi and other countries still celebrate the fruit of that mighty revival today. The anthem 'Tukutendereza Yesu' is still sung with nostalgic ecstasy.

Between 1959 and 1963, the cradle of the revival was rocked by a bloody ethnic massacre that left more than 30,000 people dead, and 100,000 refugees. Roads trekked by missionaries and revival teams were now trodden by refugees. The church had been growing, while atrocities and injustices also grew. Churches complied with government policies on 'ethnic equilibrium'. Between 1990 and 1994, ethnic tensions were once more growing visibly . . . until a million Tutsis were brutally massacred in fewer than 100 days – often inside church buildings, and with the participation of clergy. So what had gone wrong with our Christianity?

An autopsy of the church failure
Many factors contributed. We will look at the most obvious, before drawing lessons for the future.

The content of the message: a partial, selective gospel
The message received was not contextualized to the needs and problems of the nation. Missionaries had found a unified nation with three groups: Hutus, Tutsis and Twas, the power being in the hands of the Tutsi monarchy. These groups were more social classes than ethnic groups, and discernible seeds of evil already existed in their relationships: inequalities in power distribution, negative social stereotypes, contempt for the poor, and other social ills. Rather than correcting these, colonial authorities and missionaries built upon them, favouring

This work of God in repentance had not been nurtured.

the Tutsis over the other two groups. During the revival, people had repented of contempt and lack of love between different ethnic groups, and even between missionaries and the local population, but as we see in retrospect, this work of God in repentance had not been nurtured.

The methods of presentation: intellectual versus experiential

African spirituality in general, and Rwandan spirituality in particular, are experiential, always linked to personal, family and national life. In African spirituality, everything is linked: the living and the dead, the animal kingdom and the inanimate world. The world is one. There is no dichotomy between the material, physical and visible, and the spiritual and invisible. Yet Christianity was presented intellectually, with the memorization of verses and catechism, not touching experientially on issues of daily life.

Many of those baptized and integrated into churches found answers to daily problems in ancestral religion, and traditional perceptions defined their ethnic, racial and tribal identities and relationships. Their worldview had never been challenged, so when conflict came, people did not rely on their Christian faith, but on 'what their fathers had told them'.

The problem of the messengers: talking love, sowing divisions

The Catholic missionaries kept blocking the advance of other Christian denominations in the country, sometimes using new converts in acts of violence. This created more divisions and animosity among the people; they did not see Christianity as a unifying factor, but as another colonial import.

The relationship between church and politics

From the colonial period, the church in Rwanda, mainly the Roman Catholic Church, worked hand in hand with the political leaders, often influencing their decisions. This prevented the church from keeping a critical distance in order to raise a prophetic voice when needed.

Rediscovering the gospel of reconciliation

After the 1994 genocide, the church was covered in shame and sat on the bench with the accused. Many questions were thrown at her. How could such a thing happen in a country that was almost 90% Christian? Would Rwanda turn away from Christianity, become Muslim even? The opposite has happened. Between 1994 and 2002, Christianity grew by 4%, and now represents 95% of the population. We are called Christians, but we still have problems. So the question today is: has anything changed? Answer: yes and no! We now know the message we should preach to heal the wounds of our nation. But those who preach it are not doing it with intentionality – that is, preaching it until we see change!

Here are six aspects of the healing message we have rediscovered:

1. A new perspective on sin and alienation

When sin entered the world in Genesis 3, man was separated from God, separated from himself (psychological problems), separated from his neighbour (social problems) and separated from nature (ecological problems). Those four levels of alienation are present wherever you find sin. If we are to preach the message of reconciliation to communities, we need to rediscover that message about sin, for sin is the dividing factor in every situation.

2. A new perspective on preaching Christ crucified: Isaiah 53:4–6

We have rediscovered the power of preaching Christ and him crucified. We often preach Christ as our sin-bearer, but forget he is also our pain-bearer. Christ takes the sins of the offenders and the pain of the offended, and he brings us together and reconciles us. That's the message we need to preach in divided countries.

  a. Our pain-bearer. Christ, our sin-bearer, calls people to offload their pain, frustrations, anger, hatred and bitterness on the cross. This is the message the offended must hear in order to be healed. It is only when people have been healed that they can forgive.

b. Our sin-bearer. This is often preached in an abstract way, covering all doctrinal truth, but without touching on those issues of perpetrators and offenders. When preached pertinently, this message leads the offender to confess and repent. As well as finding reconciliation with God through Christ, the offender will be helped to find reconciliation with others of different factions.

c. Our reconciler (Ephesians 2:11–22). It is only when the offender asks for forgiveness, and when the offended has been healed and is ready to forgive, that real reconciliation happens. And at the cross of Jesus Christ is the place for this to happen.

3. A new perspective on our identity: 2 Corinthians 5:17

We must help people see the influences that made them what they are: legacies of their human condition, their native continent, country, region and family, as well as their personal problems. Our old bitter roots yield the bitter fruit of the flesh (Galatians 5:19–21). But when we help people with the message of the cross to rediscover their identity in Christ, to rediscover that they are new creations when they come to Christ, they will start growing new roots and new fruit: the fruit of the Spirit, rather than the fruit of the flesh.

4. A new perspective on the mission of the church: 2 Corinthians 5:18

Once the church starts to preach this message, we become ambassadors of reconciliation between God and man, and between man and man: 'God . . . gave us the ministry of reconciliation.' As you know, I sit on the National Unity and Reconciliation Commission in my country, but before the government put me on that commission, Jesus put me in the ministry of reconciliation, preaching Christ whose Spirit converts people and transforms nations.

5. A new perspective on social relationships: the holy nation of God

In Christ Jesus, we are a holy nation of God. We are not Hutus or Tutsis or Twa; nor are we white or black or yellow. Ethnic, racial and gender divisions are all against the spirit of the gospel (Galatians 3:26–28).

6. A new perspective on the power of our unity: mission and reconciliation

Our mission will be credible when we are united. Jesus said, 'People will know that you are my disciples, if you have love for one another' (John 13:35). He prayed that his disciples might be one, 'so that the world may know that you sent me' (John 17:23). Only then will people know we are Jesus' disciples and accept him as their Saviour. Jesus said that, when the church of Christ lives in love and unity, great things will happen in our nations. This is what we need to rediscover. 'There the LORD has commanded the blessing' (Psalm 133:3).

So what lessons can we draw from the Rwanda experience?

We need to re-examine the evangelization and discipleship of our own nations. We need to analyse the past and present, identify areas of woundedness and alienation, and prepare teaching that can lead to healing and reconciliation. Our nations are broken, but we can heal them with the message of the gospel.

Very often we take it for granted that, if we preach, people come to Christ, their wounds are gone and they are new people. That's not true. We need to preach this message intentionally and repeti- tively until we see things happening and people changing.

We need to accept our calling as 'ministers of reconciliation', and accept responsibility if we preach and our communities still remain wounded and full of hatred. We are here to change the world, and the Lord has given us this message. Let's go out and preach it, and let reconciliation become a lifestyle rather than a programme.

Antoine Rutayisire is Dean of the Anglican Cathedral of Kigali. He has served as General Secretary of the Union des Groupes Bibliques Universitaires du Rwanda (IFES) and as Team Leader of Africa Evangelistic Enterprise, Rwanda.

ETHNICITY IN THE MISSION OF GOD[1]
Dewi Hughes (UK)

Peace to the nations (Zechariah 9:10)

When we think of words such as 'ethnic', 'ethnicity' or 'ethnic identity', we often associate them with 'conflict', and many evangelicals consider ethnicity a divisive part of human identity. But ethnic identity is a gift from God. Some definitions may be helpful.

Ethnicity: The transliteration of the Greek plural of *ethnos* is *ethnē*, translated as 'nations' or 'Gentiles' in English Bibles. I will use *ethnos* (singular) and *ethnē* (plural) as English nouns.
Ethnos: A type of community conscious of being a people distinct from others and with a common proper name; a common ancestry; shared history and memories of a common past; elements of a common culture, such as language, customs, religion; a link with a homeland; a sense of solidarity.
Ethnic minorities: *Ethnē* that for various reasons, such as migration or enforced transportation (slavery), are dispersed in a state.
National minorities or *indigenous peoples*: *Ethnē* that have been oppressed or marginalized in their ancestral territory.

In light of these definitions, the term 'nation' becomes problematic. For example, many call the United Kingdom a 'nation', while really it is a country or state made up of three national minorities (indigenous peoples), a dominant national majority and many ethnic minorities. According to these definitions, a 'nation state' – implying a state ruling over an individual nation – hardly exists at all. Korea (North and South) and Lesotho are rare examples of states that have almost the same boundaries as an individual *ethnos*.

The overwhelming majority of the world's states have many *ethnē*, although in many multi-ethnic states one *ethnos* is dominant.

Ethnē in modern thought

According to Western modernist historians and political philosophers, the pattern of nation states emerged when, in th   hteenth
century, Enlightenment political philosophy was put   actice
in the formation of the USA and post-revolutionary Fra.... . These
new nation states offered equality to engage in the political process,
and freedom to engage in economic activity. Suppressing ethnic
distinctions was part of the price that people believed had to be
paid. In the USA, freedom and equality were denied to Native
Americans as Native Americans. In France, the Bretons and Basques,
for example, who had preserved their identity within the monarchi-
cal French state, were brutally suppressed by the brotherhood of
revolutionaries. The same pattern was followed as other European
states adopted the Enlightenment philosophy. In the United
Kingdom, there was a renewed move to suppress Irish, Scottish and
Welsh identity.

Up to the middle of the twentieth century, eliminating ethnic
distinctiveness was seen as altruistic, as diversity was 'a hindrance'
to a democratic industrialized society. If people's primary needs were
physical, then once they saw the benefits of uniformity, they would
happily jettison their ethnic identity. However, that did not happen.
This political creed on which post-colonial states were established
blamed their failure on ethnocentrism or tribalism.

Since the mid-twentieth century, the modernist paradigm,
especially in Western countries, has been changing. Multicultural-
ism has superseded as state policy in many countries. In Europe,
this has led to a measure of autonomy for some indigenous *ethnē*,
such as Catalans in Spain and Scots in the UK. This could well be
the beginning of a postmodernist paradigm of the nation state
in the West.

Ethnē in the biblical story of God's mission

The biblical book of origins (Genesis 1 – 11) ends with an account
of the origins of the *ethnē* (Genesis 10:1 – 11:9). In Genesis 10, the
existence of *ethnē* is seen as a direct result of the outworking of

God's command to the original human beings to multiply and fill
the earth (Genesis 1:28). The fulfilling of this command is twice
interrupted. The first interruption is the flood that destroys most
of humanity. After the flood, God reasserts his command to 'be
fruitful and increase in number' and 'multiply on the earth and
increase upon it' (Genesis 9:7). The evidence that this command
was effective is found in the table of nations in Genesis 10. As the
families of Noah's sons grew, economic and other pressures drove
some clans to go in search of a new place where they would be better
off. Very early in the history of humanity, some even crossed the
sea in this search,[2] so that in time distinct peoples came into existence
and 'spread out into their territories, by their clans within their
nations, each with their own language'.[3]

It is interesting that the 'nations' of Genesis 10 correspond
closely to the main features of *ethnē*. Many of the names in Genesis
10 are somewhere between a proper name for an ethnic group and
the name of an ancestor. For example, Japheth's son Gomer is a
proper name of an Indo-European people who lived in southern
Russia; and Madai or Medes is the proper name of an Indo-Iranian
people.[4] In verses 8–12, there is a break in the genealogy to tell the
story of Nimrod, one of the descendants of Cush, the son of Ham,
who was the founder of Babylon and Nineveh in Mesopotamia.
This is a good example of the type of historical memory that forms
an ethnic identity. The diversity of languages following the scattering
is mentioned after the genealogy of each son of Noah, while a
number of names listed are also the names of territories: Mizraim/
Egypt, Seba, Havilah and Dedan are all examples. The only specific
feature not clearly mentioned in Genesis 10 is a sense of solidarity
– but where the other five factors exist, solidarity is inevitable.

The account of the formation of *ethnē* in Genesis 10 is completed
by the story of the tower of Babel in Genesis 11:1–9. Events at Babel
tell us that what seemed to be a perfectly 'natural' process in Genesis
10 was in fact deeply affected by human wickedness. After the flood,
human beings with one common language start moving east from
Ararat until they come to the broad and fertile plain of Mesopotamia.

There they settle down and multiply in number and skills. To make a name for themselves, they set about building a tower reaching to heaven. This is probably the first proclamation of empire in human history: a city seeking to dominate the rest of humanity, and usurp a position that belongs to God alone.

The city and its tower were to be a magnetic centre of power that would keep people from moving outwards and filling the earth, as God had intended. And a united humanity with one language would have an endless capacity for rebellion, so God confused their language, thus hindering their ability to communicate freely and work together in opposition to God's will. So the tower was abandoned as humanity scattered 'over the face of all the earth' (11:9). The final outcome was precisely what God had originally intended for the human race: that is, for the whole earth to be filled with people of ethnic diversity. Genesis 10 and 11 together suggest that the formation of different *ethnē* was a part of God's providence, but that this process was marred by sin, like everything else since the fall.

> **This is probably the first proclamation of empire in human history.**

There is a striking contrast between the story of the tower of Babel and the beginning of the story of redemption, in the call and life of Abraham. The Babylonians set out to make their own name great, and were prepared to hinder the development of *ethnē* to achieve their end. By contrast, God would make Abraham's name great, and in the process bring blessing to the nations. The oppression or elimination of *ethnē* is the way of Babel: the complete antithesis of the blessing God intends for them through Abraham's seed, Jesus.

Passages such as Deuteronomy 2:9–12, 19–23; 32:8; Jeremiah 18:1–10 and 27:1–7 testify to God's sovereign control of the *ethnē*.[5] In the New Testament, Paul affirms to the Athenian intellectuals of the Areopagus that all nations are ultimately descended from Adam, and that God has overseen, and will continue to oversee, their formation, geographical extent and demise (Acts 17:26–27). God's sovereignty over the *ethnē* means that (i) in the long view, nations are not permanent entities. They begin, grow, flourish, decline and die like human beings. Therefore, there is no room for the idolatrous absolutizing of the *ethnos* as happens in ideological nationalism. (ii) God has a moral purpose in his dealing with the *ethnē*/nations. For example, repentance can save a nation from oblivion (Jeremiah 18:7–10; Jonah 3), and one nation can be used by God to punish another nation for its sin, though that should never be used to justify acts of aggression or war against another people (Deuteronomy 9:4–5).[6]

The New Testament focuses on two additional themes with roots in the Old Testament. Nations are invited to welcome the good news of the kingdom of God. See the prophetic introduction to this in Deuteronomy 2, as the nations in the last days flock to Zion to present their gifts to God.[7] The climax of this Old Testament prophecy is then seen in John's New Testament vision of heavenly glory in Revelation 21:24 – 22:5. As a counterpoint theme, the nations conspire together to destroy the kingdom of God. The book of Revelation, again echoing Old Testament prophecy, pictures this as the battle of Armageddon, a final struggle between a worldly empire that destroys *ethnē* and the kingdom of the Lamb that blesses *ethnē*. Until that final conflict, there should be no doubt about our aspirations as followers of the Lamb – we should bless and not destroy *ethnē*.

In Revelation 7:9, we have a beautiful picture of what the Bible teaches nations. John sees people from every nation, tribe, people and language, dressed in white robes, standing before the throne of the Lamb. All *ethnē* will be united in Jesus and his justice/righteousness. But this unity will not destroy their distinctiveness, for they will be honoured and distinguished as members of different nations/ *ethnē*. In Jesus the Messiah, we have a unity that does not destroy diversity, and a diversity that does not undermine unity.

Ethnē in modern evangelical missionary theory and practice

There is no coherent biblical view of ethnicity/nationhood in current evangelical missiology. The frequent condemnation of nationalism/ tribalism by evangelical leaders is evidence of the acceptance of modernist political philosophy, whereas the continuing drive to

translate the Bible into all languages shows missionary practice
cutting right across this philosophy.

In a modern nation state, ethnic diversity is supposed to disappear
in the wake of human equality and prosperity. Many Christians see
so-called ethnic conflicts as the reason why the economic miracle
of industrialization has not happened. But the cause of the problem
could be modern political philosophy rather than ethnic identity.
Ethnocentrism is at the root of the modernist nation state. So in
Uganda, where the state can function only by retaining English as
an official language, the ethnocentrism imposed by the colonial
oppressor is found to be more palatable than any one of the Ugandan
ethnē. The possibility of building a state on the basis of mutual
respect between *ethnē* does not seem to have been considered.

As we have seen, the evangelical mission strategy of Bible translation cuts right across the modernist view of the nation state.
It asserts that communicating in a
person's own language is vital to
effective evangelism. For missionaries
to learn a person's language in order to
communicate their message gives
dignity and significance to ethnic
identity. Grammars, dictionaries and
other books have played a vital part in
the formation and survival of *ethnē/*
nations. Committing a language to

> **Evangelical mission strategy cuts right across the modernist view of the nation state.**

writing and translating the Bible truly ennobles such identity. Bible
translators give *ethnē*, however small, an enhanced possibility of
survival and growth into full nationhood. This is indeed consonant
with our call from the first scattering of God's people at Babel.

[*See overleaf for questions.*]

Questions for discussion

- How can the church model the biblical principle of unity in diversity in the context of ethnic diversity?
- How can church appointments reflect ethnic unity in diversity?
- How significant should ethnic identity be in the training of church leaders?
- Should Christians insist that the initial education of all be in their mother tongue?
- Should churches think more deeply about the relationship between ethnic identity and poverty?
- If establishing a church in an *ethnos* helps to create a greater sense of nationhood, what should a) the church and b) the mission agency do when that leads to a desire for greater political self-determination?
- Does a nation state with a free-market economic model legalize the dispossession of poor *ethnē* by rich *ethnē*?
- How does the biblical bias towards the protection of the lowest and the least apply in the context of ethnic identity (Deuteronomy 7:7)?
- How does 'love your [ethnic] neighbour as yourself' apply in a kingdom paradigm of inter-ethnic relations?

Dewi Hughes is Theological Advisor to Tearfund. www.tearfund.org

DAY 3

WORLD FAITHS: Bearing witness to the love of Christ among people of other faiths

TESTIMONY: COSTLY WITNESS AND THE GOD WHO PROTECTS
Archbishop Ben Kwashi (Nigeria)

The gospel is powerful, as is demonstrated by the death and resurrection of Jesus Christ. By that single event, we see the final defeat of Satan, of the powers of hell, of sin and of all that is evil. It is therefore no use – at any time – to be afraid of the devil, or to submit or to surrender to him, because the devil and all his powers have been defeated by Jesus Christ. Hallelujah! This is why the gospel is very powerful.

Between 7 and 12 March 1987, 100 churches in Zaire City were burned down, and over 300 Christian homes and businesses were destroyed. People died. I was the leader of the Zaire chapter of the Christian Association. The Lord asked me to tell the people to do nothing. I circulated a letter, and the Christians stood back and watched.

Three years later, I was the bishop in Jos. On the very same dates, 7–12 March 2010, in three villages on the outskirts of the city, Muslims massacred Christian men, women and children. The church leaders begged the villagers and those who had survived and the entire Christian community to do nothing. They cried until their voices and their tears dried up, and there was nothing more to cry. They just watched.

In 2006, over forty people came to my house to kill me. I had actually postponed my return home, so they met my wife. They did unspeakable things to her: they beat her and left her half dead and totally blind. Through the mercy of God, she recovered. Exactly one year later, they came back again, over thirty of them, and this time they met me at home. They broke down the back door, came in and took me outside to kill me. Then they changed their minds and said they would kill me in my bedroom. I pleaded to be able to pray, and they allowed me to do so. As I prostrated myself before the Lord, suddenly after about two minutes my wife was holding my hands. Five minutes later, my son came in, and I said, 'What are you doing here?' He said, 'Daddy, they have gone.' What chased them away – what they saw, what they didn't see – only eternity will reveal.

Now I'm not saying this to play down what happened to those who died. I have a classmate who was a pastor in Kaduna. He was burned alive in his church. I have lost colleagues, schoolmates and brothers and sisters who have been slaughtered for the faith. Why I'm alive, I don't know. But one thing I do know: until my time is up, and I know I will die some day – blood crash, air crash, car crash, whatever crash – until that day, I have a gospel to proclaim. I have a gospel worth living for, and I have a gospel worth dying for.

Archbishop Benjamin Argak Kwashi serves as Bishop of the Anglican Diocese of Jos and Archbishop of the Ecclesiastical province of Jos.
www.anglican-nig.org

EPHESIANS 3:1–21
John Piper (USA)

Making known the manifold wisdom of God through prison and prayer

I'm going to preach this message twice. *First*, to give you the big picture of where we are going, in three scenes; *second*, to draw out implications from these three scenes for our moment in history.

Scene one

The great, sovereign, cosmic purpose of God is to make known the glory of his wisdom to the powers of the universe (verses 8–10):[1]

> To me, though I am the very least of all the saints, this grace was given, to preach to the Gentiles the unsearchable riches of Christ, and to bring to light for everyone what is the plan of the mystery hidden for ages in God who created all things, *so that* through the church the manifold wisdom of God might now be made known to the rulers and authorities in the heavenly places.

God gave Paul two things to do: preach the unsearchable riches of Christ, and make known the mysterious plan of God hidden for ages. What was God's great cosmic purpose in this?

We know from Ephesians 6:12 that these 'rulers and authorities' are demonic powers. We do not wrestle against flesh and blood; we wrestle against the devil and his messengers.

The cosmic purpose of God is to make the whole universe say, 'God is infinitely wise!' The preaching of the unsearchable riches of Christ and the revelation of the mysterious plan of God have this one ultimate purpose: to make known the glory of his wisdom to the demonic powers of the universe.

God is not a tribal deity. His purposes encompass the whole universe. If there had been humans on other planets in other galaxies, they would have been invited to Lausanne. We are not merely a global congress on *world* evangelization. We are a global congress on the cosmic manifestation of the glory of the wisdom of the Creator of the universe.

Scene two

God has ordained that some of his servants be imprisoned and suffer, as a way of bringing about God's cosmic purpose to manifest his wisdom.

We read in verse 1: 'For this reason I, Paul, a prisoner for Christ Jesus on behalf of you Gentiles', and in verse 13: 'So I ask you not to lose heart over what I am suffering for you, which is your glory.'

Paul does not mention his sufferings to attract pity, but because he wants the church to know that this is their glory.

In other words, God's design is that his church be drawn into the glory of the unsearchable riches of Christ through the sufferings of her missionaries and her ministers. Our sufferings are their glory. They are made glorious through our sufferings. Why would God glorify his church this way?

Because he is infinitely, gloriously wise. And he means for all heaven and hell to see this through his church.

Scene three

God has chosen that the supernatural power required to see the glory of his wisdom, and to suffer for his name, will come through earnest prayer (verses 14–21).

Paul is praying throughout these verses that what he is preaching will in fact happen. Notice the connection between verse 14 and all that has gone before:

- Paul wants us to see and enjoy the unsearchable riches of Christ (verse 8)
- Paul wants us to understand and embrace the mystery hidden for ages (verse 9)

- Paul wants us to be a part of revealing the glory of God's wisdom to the powers of darkness (verse 10)
- And Paul wants his own suffering to be our glory (verse 13)

So he says in verse 14, '*For this reason* I bow my knees before the Father.' Why? Because:

- No human being can see the riches of Christ – the breadth and length and height and depth of it all
- No human being can embrace the mystery of the ages
- No-one can reveal the glory of God's wisdom
- No-one can be transformed from one degree of glory to the next through suffering, without omnipotent, divine, supernatural power. And God has chosen to give that power to his church through prayer.

Here are some implications. Again, let's look at three scenes.

Round two: scene one
This has three parts:

- The demonstration of the *wisdom of God* to the powers of darkness (verse 10)
- The preaching of the unsearchable *riches of Christ* (verse 8)
- The revelation of the *mystery* hidden in God (verse 9)

How do they relate to one another?

Notice what the *mystery* is. It's defined in verse 6: 'This mystery is that the Gentiles [the nations – that's most of us] are fellow heirs, members of the same body, and partakers of the promise in Christ Jesus through the gospel.'

The mystery is that the Gentiles – every tribe and language and people and nation – will now be included in all the promises God made to Israel. This is why verse 8 says that Paul preaches to the Gentiles – the nations – the unsearchable riches of Christ, the

Messiah. All the promises of God made in the Old Testament belong now to the Messiah Jesus and to his people (2 Corinthians 1:20).

So now we have connected two parts of scene one: the mystery hidden for ages is that all the peoples of the world will be included in the unsearchable riches of the Messiah. God will bring them to life and to faith, he will forgive their sins, declare them righteous in his sight, give them his Spirit; make them holy, raise them from the dead, reign over them in righteousness, banish all evil and suffering from the world, and make them everlastingly happy with him in the new heaven and the new earth.

So if the mystery is the inclusion of the nations in the unsearchable riches of the Messiah, then how does this relate to the manifestation of the wisdom of God? This mystery is 'through the gospel' (verse 6).

Paul's clearest definition of the gospel goes like this: 'Now I would remind you of the gospel . . . that Christ died for our sins in accordance with the Scriptures, that he was buried, that he was raised on the third day in accordance with the Scriptures' (1 Corinthians 15:1, 3–4).

So we Gentiles are included in the riches of the Messiah because he died for us, bore our sins, completed our righteousness and conquered our death and hell and the devil. As Ephesians 2:16 says, he reconciled us to God by his cross.

In Paul's mind, how does the cross relate to *the wisdom of God*? The resounding answer is given in 1 Corinthians 1:22–24:

Jews demand signs and Greeks seek *wisdom*, but we preach
Christ crucified, a stumbling block to Jews and folly to
Gentiles, but to those who are called, both Jews and Greeks,
Christ the power of God and *the wisdom of God*.

The crucifixion is not the world's wisdom, not the world's power. It is foolishness and weakness to the world. But it is *God's power*. And it is *God's wisdom*. When the Messiah dies on the cross to create the church out of all the nations of the world, the manifold wisdom of

God shines most brightly in that very crucified Messiah: 'Christ the power of God and the wisdom of God'.

But here is an amazing thing. The rulers and authorities don't just see the wisdom of God at the cross. They see it in *what the cross created*, namely the church, from every people, tribe and nation.

'*Through the church* the manifold wisdom of God might now be made known to the rulers and authorities in the heavenly places' (verse 10). There isn't anything greater that can be said of the global church of Christ than that Christ died so that she would be the display of God's infinite wisdom.

So scene number one is the inclusion of the Gentile nations in the unsearchable riches of the Messiah through the gospel of Christ crucified in our place. And that crucifixion is the wisdom of God displayed in the creation of a redeemed people from every tribe and language and nation. One day all rulers, all authorities, all demons and Satan himself, as they are cast into the lake of fire, will be forced to say, 'God is infinitely wise.'

So why did the Son of God have to be crucified for the Jewish people, and the nations to be included in the unsearchable riches of Christ? 'We all once lived in the passions of our flesh, carrying out the desires of the body and the mind, and were *by nature children of wrath*, like the rest of mankind' (Ephesians 2:3).

All mankind, Paul says, are 'children of wrath' apart from faith in Christ. Because of our sinful rebellious nature, we are under the wrath of God. This is why Christ had to die. Not just because we were sinners, but because he is holy. His infinite justice demanded that he punish sinners.

If God had not put Christ forward to bear his own wrath, if Christ had not become a curse for us, as Galatians 3:13 says, then all the nations and all Jews would have perished under God's wrath and entered into everlasting suffering in hell, as Jesus said in Matthew 25:46.

I draw out this implication of the cross to hold together two truths that are often felt to be at odds with each other, but which belong together: (i) that when the gospel takes root in our souls, it impels us out, towards the alleviation of all unjust suffering in this age. That's what love does! (ii) that when the gospel takes root in our souls, it awakens us to the horrible reality of eternal suffering in hell, under the wrath of a just and omnipotent God. And it impels us to rescue the perishing, and to warn people to flee from the wrath to come (1 Thessalonians 1:10).

I plead with you. Don't choose between those two truths. Embrace them both. It doesn't mean that we will all spend our time in the same way. God forbid. But it means we will let the Bible define reality and define love. Could Lausanne say – could the evangelical church say – we Christians care about all suffering, especially eternal suffering? I hope we can say that. But if we feel resistant to saying, 'especially eternal suffering', or resistant to saying, 'We care about all suffering in this age', then either we have a defective view of hell or a defective heart. I pray that Lausanne would have neither.

Round two: scenes two and three

God appoints *suffering* and *prayer* as means of gathering the nations into the unsearchable riches of Christ for the glory of his infinite wisdom.

'So I ask you not to lose heart over what I am suffering for you, which is your glory' (verse 13). When Paul was willing to go to prison for the sake of Christ, he showed the nations that Christ is more precious than freedom. When he was willing to suffer for Christ, he showed the nations that Christ is more precious than comfort and security and prosperity. In other words, the infinite value of the unsearchable riches of Christ shines brightly not in Paul's prosperity, but in his imprisonment. With his suffering, he draws the nations towards the glory of Christ and displays the wisdom of the cross.

But no-one chooses prison, no-one turns from prosperity, no-one sees the breadth and length and height and depth of the love of Christ that passes knowledge, no-one is filled with all the fullness of God, and no-one says, 'I count everything as loss for the sake of

Christ', without supernatural, omnipotent power coming into their lives. And as Paul shows us, this comes by prayer.

Most of the peoples of the world where the church is not yet planted don't want us to bring the gospel. But they will perish if it does not reach them. If, for Christ's sake, we are willing to go – and Christ commands this – then we *will* suffer. And if our suffering is to be the glory of the world, then we must pray for that.

'So to you, O Lord, who is able to do far more abundantly than all that we ask or think, according to the power at work within us, to you be glory in the church and in Christ Jesus throughout all generations, for ever and ever. Amen' (Ephesians 3:20–21).

John Piper is Pastor for Preaching and Vision at Bethlehem Baptist Church, Minneapolis, Minnesota, and author of over forty books.
www.desiringGod.org

THE GOSPEL, THE GLOBAL CHURCH AND THE WORLD OF ISLAM
Nour Armagan* (Middle East)

Unlike the vast majority of Muslims who decided to follow Christ, I didn't have a 'supernatural' conversion. I was seventeen when I went to a local Anglican church in my country of origin, because of erroneous reports in a local newspaper that the church gave US$100 every Sunday to Muslim visitors, served wine, and lured them to become Christian with promises of attractive women and visas to Europe. Sadly, the deal never worked out! The elderly expatriate congregation had no eligible candidate for romance, did not allow us to drink wine, and even took money from us.

Some fourteen years have passed since that Sunday, and so much has happened. But I am still confident of the gospel of Jesus of Nazareth, now more than ever. Not in a sentimental or sadly even in a childlike way, but following years of personal anguish and struggle. I have worked through the misery of feeling homeless and not belonging, facing pain; struggling in my commitment to academic rigour as an act of worship; plus the darkness, as a human rights researcher, of witnessing first-hand the suffering of God's children. For every prayer of praise in my life, there are ten times more prayers of anger, weariness and tears.

In other words, I am an earthly man with no saintly claims, trapped between the fault-lines of this world, between the imagined boundaries of the West and East, and most painfully between Christendom and Islam. And from where I stand, I see three major failures that hinder the global church from facing two of its biggest challenges today: Islam and the future of the church in the Muslim-majority world.

The *first* is the failure to understand the nature of the world in which we live, and develop a Christ-like response to it. Often the word 'Islam' is used to refer to a diverse range of issues, countries, cultures, politics and historical eras. This unification of disconnected realities fools us into thinking that we are facing a monolithic and timeless entity, one which can be understood simply, by reading verses in the Qur'an. Within such narratives, the individual Muslim is effaced and dehumanized, and seen not as a bearer of the image of God, but of the image of whatever we think we are not. Such faulty understandings of Islam and Muslims give legitimacy to ethnocentrism, fear, prejudice and exclusion. This makes Muslims today's Sadducees – despised and feared by the Pharisees of our day, but dearly loved by Christ, enough for him to give his life for them.

The *second* failure is in not realizing that the know-how of the modern mission movement was a product of the twentieth century, and is now outmoded. At a theological level, inadequate perceptions of the gospel (e.g. individuals going to heaven, happy middle-class lives being enhanced by personal holiness, or personal experiences of the Holy Spirit) cannot cope with the complex reality of the twenty-first century. These perceptions lead only to clichéd formulations of gospel truth, which are out of tune with their intended audience. They have no objective reference points beyond their Christian sub-culture, though their proponents do not see this.

At a practical level, the era of (i) smuggling Bibles, (ii) reducing the gospel to smart tracts and cunning distribution, (iii) raising support for expatriate missionaries living in faraway lands, and (iv) safari-style short-term mission trips ended in the mid-twentieth century. It has been superseded, just as old-style technologies used for building hospitals and schools have been superseded. However, the tendency to confuse methods of promoting the gospel with the gospel itself remains a common fallacy. Being faithful in declaring the gospel is too often equated with continuing methodologies or metaphors developed in a previous century.

Changes in the Islamic world since the 9/11 attacks on the World Trade Center demand a completely new way of thinking about missions, making most of what we have been doing counterproductive.

The *third* failure is misunderstanding the situation of the church in the Muslim world. There is a thirst for miraculous conversion

stories, but not for a mature grasp of what is happening. People think
in terms of leading a Muslim to Christ as a one-off event, without
considering what happens next. In the majority of the Islamic world,
around 80% of new followers of Christ give up on their new faith
after two years, and by the fifth year only a small proportion remain
as Christians. Those who do remain are often trapped in small
enclaves, with hardly any testimony outside a local church. The
common myth that the church always grows under persecution passes
without challenge, when by and large the church in the Islamic world
is fading away or exiled to social peripheries, with no voice in the
larger society. This is happening even though there is an emerging
church made up of Muslim-background believers in certain places.
Our longing to hear magical stories of large-scale conversions is
blinding us from seeing the suffering of millions of Christians, and
stopping us from running to their help.

If this critique of failure is correct, then to be faithful to the One
we worship we need to start all over again. We need to have the
courage to ask afresh the questions every generation must ask for
itself. What does it mean to believe in and follow Jesus of Nazareth?
What does the cross say to a world polarized in a language of 'us'
versus 'them'? What does it mean to believe in a Messiah who is
fully divine and fully human, in an age when human beings can be
killed by unmanned drones operated from offices thousands of miles
away? Does the fact that Jesus was an asylum seeker in a neighbouring country have anything to say to more than 40 million refugees,
asylum seekers and stateless persons in the world today? They are
so often disparaged and suffer serious abuses. What does it mean to
be Christ's body in a world full of hate, caught up in the politics of
fear, and with many cultural clashes?

Only when we have engaged with these basic questions can we
endeavour to ask the 'how' questions. For we need to know how to
communicate the reason for our hope to a deaf world, unwilling
to listen to us.

The future of the gospel in the Islamic world rests with the
Muslim-background church. It must be equipped with a theology

firmly based on the cross, engaging with the realities of the context in which it is placed. We must look to God for a new breed of Christian leaders, writers, intellectuals, artists and prophets who will fight for, and win, respect, as they raise their voices publicly in matters of culture and take their places in policy-forming circles. Only then will the Christian message be heard through the present thick curtains of prejudice; only then will Christians be seen as plausible members of society, with something important to say.

May we boldly, lovingly and wisely declare Christ's name to this dark and weary world.

The fate of the church in the Islamic world is also undoubtedly tied in with how the global church, particularly the Western church, interacts with Islam and Muslims. The church in the Islamic world cannot speak with credibility about love, redemption and reconciliation, while Christians in other parts of the world fail to demonstrate these towards Muslims living among them, and do not challenge foreign policies in their countries when they contradict Christian values.

May we boldly, lovingly and wisely continue to declare Christ's name to this dark and weary world, and lift up his cross, so that our generation too might look at it and be saved by it.

*A pseudonym, for security reasons.
Nour Armagan is a Middle Eastern theologian and activist.

BEARING WITNESS TO CHRIST'S LOVE AMONG THOSE OF OTHER FAITHS
Michael Ramsden (UK)

And what more shall I say? For time would fail me to tell of Gideon, Barak, Samson, Jephthah, of David and Samuel and the prophets – who through faith conquered kingdoms, enforced justice, obtained promises, stopped the mouths of lions, quenched the power of fire, escaped the edge of the sword, were made strong out of weakness, became mighty in war, put foreign armies to flight. Women received back their dead by resurrection. Some were tortured, refusing to accept release, so that they might rise again to a better life. Others suffered mocking and flogging, and even chains and imprisonment. They were stoned, they were sawn in two, they were killed with the sword. They went about in skins of sheep and goats, destitute, afflicted, mistreated – of whom the world was not worthy – wandering about in deserts and mountains, and in dens and caves of the earth.

And all these, though commended through their faith, did not receive what was promised, since God had provided something better for us, that apart from us they should not be made perfect.

Therefore, since we are surrounded by so great a cloud of witnesses, let us also lay aside every weight, and sin which clings so closely, and let us run with endurance the race that is set before us, looking to Jesus, the founder and perfecter of our faith, who for the joy that was set before him endured the cross, despising the shame, and is seated at the right hand of the throne of God.
(Hebrews 11:32 – 12:2)

Love is costly. Out of love, something may be given for nothing, but that does not mean it costs the giver nothing. It may cost everything. When it comes to witnessing to people of other faiths, we seem to look for methods that cost us nothing. But love always costs. Rejected love is painful – Jesus himself expressed his heartfelt longing in the face of stubborn rejection. There is an urgent need for us to pour out our lives in reaching the lost, as he poured out his life and reached down to us. E. M. Bounds famously remarked that, as the world is looking for better methods, God is looking for better men. Perhaps we need to concentrate on changing our hearts more than on working on our methods.

In preparing his disciples for the trials of this world, Jesus told them that difficulty would come. They might have thought that, with God on their side, no suffering would befall them. But Jesus warned, 'I have said all these things to you to keep you from falling away. They will put you out of the synagogues. Indeed, the hour is coming when whoever kills you will think that he is offering service to God' (John 16:1–2).

Immediately before this, Jesus says, 'And you also will bear witness . . . ' (John 15:27). The word 'witness' is from the Greek word *martys*, which has travelled down church history, and from which comes the word 'martyr'. Even in the New Testament, the connection between being a witness and suffering is very clear. We are all called to be witnesses. In being a faithful witness to Christ, we will suffer persecution: 'If they persecuted me, they will also persecute you' (John 15:20). 'The world . . . hated me,' Christ said (John 15:18), and so we should not be surprised at the hatred that we ourselves attract on account of his name (John 15:21). As we read in Hebrews, faith and faithfulness lead both to great victories in Christ's name – kingdoms conquered, justice enforced, promises obtained, mouths of lions stopped – and also to great cost, as the world would see it – some tortured, others mocked, flogged, in chains and imprisoned. Christians were stoned, sawn in two, killed with the sword. Truly they were those of whom the world was not worthy.

So let us set aside any thoughts of being able to witness to Christ without cost. We see great miracles – some escaping the sword, and great martyrdoms – but many killed by the sword. There is no contradiction here, just the certain knowledge that we are called to give our lives in his service and will one day be called home.

We follow in the footsteps of the *martys*, the witnesses, who went before us. They are not few; they are a great cloud. The stands they occupy are not sparsely filled – they are packed, with those who laid down their lives in the service of the Author of life, and who now have eternal life through the founder and perfecter of their faith. Let us not lose heart, nor lose our way. Rather, fixing our eyes on Christ, let us run after him who despised the shame of the cross, and is now seated at the right hand of God. Let us fix our eyes on things above.

All through history there has been a cost to evangelism. It is a cost many may not be prepared to pay. But it is this context in which the gospel took root and spread. Preaching a message of repentance and faith has always been challenging. I have had the privilege of speaking in countries where personal safety cannot be guaranteed. It is always disappointing to hear concerns that maybe I shouldn't go because the risks are too great. Our goal is not to preserve our lives at any cost, but to live in obedience to the call we have received. Of course, we are not called to ignore risk, and everything must be considered prayerfully. But to refuse God's call because of hardship? The first apostles would struggle to recognize that as genuine Christian obedience.

There are several pointers for us in Hebrews:

- *Travel lightly.* Don't be held up by the weight of sin or the weariness that comes from the world. Have we let the things of this world weigh us down?
- *Be aware.* Watch out for the sin that so easily entangles us and clings to us, slowing us down and eventually tripping us up. Are we spiritually alert and alive?
- *Run.* Run the race with endurance. This is not a quick sprint. We are running a marathon. Are we in danger of collapsing before the end, without pacing our life in a God-honouring way?
- *Focus.* Fix your eyes on Christ. Don't be distracted – that so easily leads to despair – but instead keep your eyes fixed on

the One who is with us now, and will be for eternity. There is only one gospel we have to preach – are we looking to God or to man?

- *Rejoice.* Christ looked forward to the cross with joy, not that it was going to be a pleasant experience. Rejoice in the fact that, though outwardly we may waste away, inwardly we are being renewed. If we run well, there is much to look forward to, even in the face of death: 'Some were tortured, refusing to accept release, so that they might rise again to a better life' (Hebrews 11:35).

I have not talked about prayer and proclamation, Scripture and the Holy Spirit, Christ and the cross. These are the means, the content, the power, the goal of the message. We must understand them in the light of the gospel, and we must be prepared to follow in the footsteps of those who have gone before us in obedience to God's mission.

For the early church, everyone else was by definition of 'another faith'. So we learn much just by reading the New Testament.

Two more things:

First, faithful witness often entails suffering and persecution, and there are three marks of these biblical witnesses: (i) they are passionate about the case they seek to present, and have an inner conviction of its truth. Like their first-century predecessors, they cannot but speak of what they have seen and heard; (ii) they are held accountable for the truthfulness of their testimony. Perjury is a serious, punishable offence. Sensing his solemn responsibility to speak truthfully, the apostle Paul four times declares, 'God is my witness'; (iii) they must be faithful not only to the facts of the Christ-event, but also to its meaning.[2]

Secondly, we must give thought to our own credibility as witnesses. If an eyewitness to an event has a reputation for drinking, his testimony will be questioned. We are known by our fruit. Titus 2:14 tells us that the 'purpose of Christ's death was to purify for himself a people enthusiastic for good works'.[3] Good works are not the basis of our salvation, but evidence of it; by them our gospel is 'adorned and commended to others'.[4]

The writers of *The Lausanne Covenant* wrestled with the balance between good works and the preached Word of the gospel. These two always go together, and we do well to reflect on the balance the *Covenant* expressed:

> The church may evangelize [preach the gospel]; but will the world hear and heed its message? Not unless the church retains its own integrity, the covenant insists. We must practise what we preach . . . In particular, the cross must be as central to our lives as it is to our message. Do we preach Christ crucified (1 Corinthians 1:23)? A church which preaches the cross must itself be marked by the cross.[5]

If what we preach is not evidenced in our lives, we will be seen as offering mere theory and speculation when the world is looking for transformation. We must not spring into action without sinking our roots more deeply in our understanding of the gospel. Without deep roots, the church withers.

A church which preaches the cross must itself be marked by the cross.

Are we prepared for the cost? I pray we will all learn to be true witnesses.

Michael Ramsden, European Director of RZIM Zacharias Trust, is lecturer in Christian apologetics at Wycliffe Hall, Oxford, where his main involvement is with the Oxford Centre for Christian Apologetics. www.rzim.org www.wycliffe.ox.ac.uk

DISCIPLESHIP AND MISSION IN THE AGE OF GLOBALIZATION
Os Guinness (UK) and David Wells (USA)

'Globalization' brings the greatest opportunities for mission, as well as the greatest challenges for discipleship, the church has faced since the first century. Never has the vision of 'the whole gospel for the whole world through the whole church' been closer and yet more contested.

The double-edged strength of the church

We are no longer who we were before we came to Christ, but we are not yet what we will be when Christ returns. This bracing call to tension lies at the heart of our faith. Individually and collectively, we are to live in the world in a stance of both 'yes' and 'no'; affirmation and antithesis; of being 'against the world/for the world'; in it but not of it.

This tension tests the church in every generation. When preserved, the transforming power of the Christian faith in culture has been immense, for the Christian faith is unashamedly world affirming. It has a peerless record in contributing to education, philanthropy, social reforms, medicine, the rise of science, the emergence of democracy and human rights. It has built schools, hospitals, universities, orphanages and other beneficial institutions. Yet, at the same time, it is also world denying, insisting on the place of prophets as well as priests, on sacrifice as well as fulfilment. It must expose and oppose the world wherever its attitudes and actions are against the commands of God and the interests of humanity.

The temptation has always been to relax this tension from one side or the other. Sometimes Christians have been so much in the world that they have lost their relevance to the kingdom of God. At other times, they have become so 'not of the world' that they have lost their relevance in society and have become of no earthly use.

Either way, such unfaithfulness means that the church grows weak. Unfaithfulness in the direction of worldliness is worse than weak. It brings the shadow of God's judgment.

Preserving this tension carries an inescapable implication: Christian faithfulness in any generation requires a clear-eyed understanding of the world of its day.

While the Bible uses the word 'world' of creation, our focus here is on its other use, its designation of fallen human life in its rebellion against God and his truth. Here 'world' becomes negative (e.g. 1 John 2:15–17; 5:18–19). We must understand the world if we are to witness, for communication always presupposes understanding of context. And we must understand it if we are to be aware of the danger of worldliness, for we can only avoid what we can accurately understand.

> **Christian faithfulness in any generation requires a clear-eyed understanding of the world of its day.**

The Third Lausanne Congress meets 100 years after the great world missionary conference in Edinburgh in 1910. Since then, Edinburgh's missionary vision has been gloriously vindicated. The Christian faith is global today in a way that was not true 100 years ago. Nevertheless, there was a tragic blind spot in its vision. It failed to recognize its own captivity to the powerful delusions of European 'Christendom', delusions which led to two world wars and much self-induced secularization. We today are no more omniscient than were they, but we must endeavour to be more self-critical through understanding our world and our own place in it.

Coming to terms with 'globalization'
What then is 'the world' of our day? Beyond any question, its single, strongest expression is globalization. This is the process by which human interconnectedness has expanded to a truly global level. Many people, such as the writers of *The Economist* magazine, attribute globalization to the spread of market capitalism, and use

the word only as a synonym for this expansion. But this is self-interested as well as wrong. Globalization is a multidimensional process, and the decisive driver in its present expansion is not capitalism but information technology. At the centre of the current wave of globalization are 'the triple S-forces' of speed (with the capacity for instant communication), scope (the capacity to communicate to the entire world) and simultaneity (the capacity to communicate to everywhere at the same time). Together, these forces have led to the acceleration, compression and intensification of human life on earth in the global world.

A decisive shift has taken place from the Industrial Revolution, centred on production and epitomized by the factory, to the Information Revolution, centred on communication and epitomized by the computer. There are both continuities and discontinuities with the past, and we must make our claims about the present with accuracy and humility.

The *first* task is to discern and so to make an accurate description of the realities of the world in which we find ourselves.

The *second* task is to assess and so to evaluate the pros and cons, the benefits and costs, of the world as a whole. And all must be assessed within the framework of the biblical worldview.

The *third* task is to engage and so to enter the world as disciples of Jesus, called to be salt and light, gratefully using the best of the world as gifts of God and vigilantly avoiding the worst of the world. Or, as the early church expressed it, we are to 'plunder the Egyptian gold', as the Lord told Israel to do, but we are never to set up 'a golden calf', as Israel was later judged for doing.

Easy to say, but these basic Christian tasks are harder than ever to do because of globalization. History is always more complex than we can understand, and it proceeds not by the simple influence of certain factors, but by their complicated interplay and through the ironies of their unintended consequences. Globalization only compounds our difficulty in understanding, for, by its very nature, globalization means that we who are finite now have to deal with the whole world, which is always far beyond our full comprehension.

And we are dealing with it when it is communicating and changing at an unprecedented speed. Indeed, it will have changed even before we have finished describing it.

Many of our best descriptions always require immediate reminders. *First*, globalization almost always involves two countervailing forces, and not simply one, for if the world is 'universalizing' in new ways, it is also 'localizing' in new ways (hence the new term 'glocal', to describe the impact of the global on the local and the local on the global). *Secondly*, in every new trend there are always winners and losers. Christians who honour their Master must never lose sight of the poor, the oppressed, and those left behind economically, especially those caught by the savage inequities of the globalized world. *Thirdly*, there are multiple modernities, or different ways of being modern. The old adage that 'Globalization equals Westernization equals Americanization' is both wrong and a dangerous conceit. Different cultures, with their own history and their own values, are adapting to the modern world in their own ways, and may say 'no' to what others consider 'progress'.

The global faith par excellence
Globalization has special relevance for Christians because the Christian faith has always been a global faith. We look back not just to the Great Commission, but to the promise to Abraham that he would be the father of the faithful and a blessing to the whole world. The Christian church, in fact, is the most diverse community on earth, the most multi-ethnic, the most multicultural. The Bible is the most translated book in history. This is crucial to our global perspective, a supreme fact.

Grand transformations
Globalization is transforming almost every aspect of human life. All of these transformations have a bearing on discipleship and evangelism in one way or another. Some of the major transformations that require further exploration can be summarized briefly as follows:

- Our sense of *time*, in a world of 'fast-life'. We are the first generation to live at a speed beyond our own human comprehension.
- Our sense of *place*, when space is 'compressed' and geography 'abolished'. We can communicate anywhere in the world instantly, and travel anywhere within twenty-four hours.
- Our sense of *reality*, as more and more of life is 'mediated'. The virtual replaces the natural, and face-to-face relationships give way to virtual interaction.
- Our notion of *identity*, as the fixed and enduring shifts to 'the endlessly protean'. Numerous 'identity movements' offer collective identities for those suffering from the dislocation of traditional identities.
- Our experience of *families*, as binding social ties are melting down, traditional gender roles are challenged and replaced, and the dysfunctional becomes the normal.
- Our experience of *community*, as the face-to-face shifts to the virtual and the imagined.
- Our experience of *work*, as globalization makes job security fragile.
- The place of *religion* in modern life has often been eviscerated and has become a vague 'spirituality'.
- The challenge of *other religions* and especially of 'living with our deepest differences' in the emerging 'global public square'.
- The place of *politics*, as the 'supra-national' supersedes the national, and nation states are rivalled by many global actors.
- The challenge of working toward '*global governance* without a world government'.
- The task of *leadership* in an interconnected age, as leaders now grapple with 'the whole world the whole time'.
- The nature of *knowledge*, as information explodes, generalism replaces specialization, and the internet becomes a 'garbage can' as well as a 'goldmine'.
- The power of *consumerism*, and its transformation of human desire, its drive to 'commodify' everything, turning even

sex and relationships into saleable things, and its grand
accumulation of debt and junk.

- The proliferation of *ideologies*, and especially the new ideologies
  that are rampantly pro-globalist, such as neo-liberal capitalism,
  or rampantly anti-globalist, such as 'post-colonialism'.
- Modern travel and the vast global tourist industry, which has
  spawned evils such as 'sex tourism', and modern *migration* and
  the 'manufacture of waste people', such as the millions who
  have been left homeless, identity-less, jobless, and stateless in
  refugee camps.
- Our sense of *generations*, when fast-life encourages
  'generational conceit' and the myopia that cuts itself off from
  the wisdom of the elders and the past.
- Our attitude to *tradition and change*, when novelty and fashion
  trump wisdom, custom and 'the habits of the heart'.
- The dominance of *worldwide emotions*, such as fear and the
  shameless pandering to fear-mongering and alarmism.
- The significance and scale of *globalized evil*, suffering, crime
  and oppression, and the multiple consequences for justice
  and compassion, supremely the global trafficking in sex,
  human body-parts and humans themselves.
- The exponential rise of *global side-effects*, and therefore of
  unintended consequences, unknown aftermaths.
- Our attitudes toward *the earth*, when degradation exposes its
  non-renewable fragility.
- The *prospects for the human race*, including the degradation of the
  earth, the potential destruction of the planet and extinction
  of the human species, and the question of a 'post-human
  future'.

A proper description of these profound transformations is beyond
the scope of this brief chapter. But such consequences must never
be forgotten, for they define the world in which we live and in which
we bear witness to our Lord. Our focus here is on two central areas:
globalization and discipleship, and globalization and mission.

Christian discipleship in the global era

If globalization has both local and global dimensions, and if its benefits are also trailed by extraordinary shadows, then it is a challenge to Christian discipleship. How do we think about both the benefits and the costs as Christ's followers? And how do we think of this world that lives in our consciousness at both a macro and a micro level?

- The church, if it is true to its calling, will think globally, because otherwise it will be more *parochial* than its non-Christian neighbours and, worse, untrue to its gospel calling.
- Global consciousness tends to 'relativize' and therefore diminish all absolute truth claims, because the awareness of other religions and worldviews erodes the possibility that any one of them could actually be really true.
- Capitalism and technology are uniting to produce unparalleled abundance in developed countries. In these countries, paradoxically, people have never had so much to live with and yet so little to live for. Never have they experienced such abundance through cheaply produced goods from around the world, and yet

  People have never had so much to live with and yet so little to live for.

  never have depression, anxiety and loneliness been at higher levels. And all too often, Christians in these countries are not distinguished from non-Christians in how they think about the meaning of life and what constitutes the 'good life'. This consequence of globalization is now most obvious in the West, but it will become a challenge wherever the world is modernizing.
- In a world connected electronically and virtually, the trend is to diminish face-to-face human relationships and increase 'virtual relationships' and 'social networking'. Questions are even being raised in the West as to whether anyone needs to 'go' to church any more. But could the 'church' ever be merely an 'imagined community' that exists only in the ether?

And how does this 'mediated world' impact discipleship patterned on the flesh-and-blood realities of the incarnation?

Christian mission in the global era

Increased opportunities for mission and evangelism are obvious and huge. Immigration has brought into our cities peoples from around the world. With the destruction of traditions, the collapse of traditional certainties and the meltdown of traditional roles and allegiances, there is greater political liberty, greater social fluidity, greater religious diversity and greater psychological vulnerability than ever before. As a result, human beings in the global era have been described as 'conversion prone', more open than ever to consider new faiths. So we can now spread the gospel in a way which is 'freer, faster and farther' than at any earlier time in the church's history, and we must do so with faithfulness and integrity.

We can now spread the gospel in a way which is 'freer, faster and farther'.

The following issues are examples of the challenges we must consider:

- *The political temptation*: At one extreme, more common in the West, the temptation is to see the Christian faith as the best way to defend the status quo and bolster cultures under stress. At the other, more common outside the West, it is to see the Christian faith as a variant of post-colonialism, justifying prejudice. At the same time, the pluralized world amplifies the fears surrounding the challenges of living with deep religious differences, so that religion is viewed as divisive, and evangelism as unwarranted 'proselytization'. We need to remind ourselves that 'the first thing to say about politics is that politics is not the first thing'.
- *Plausibility crisis*: Whenever the Christian faith is untrue to its own nature, it seems unlikely to outsiders that its gospel could be true.

- *The downsides of the age of communication*: We communicate with great ease, but we are also liable to succumb to the pitfalls of modern communication: the entertainment mode, the soundbite style, the sensationalist claims, the common appeal to feelings alone, the 'inflation' of ideas, the corruption of sources. To the extent that Christians use modern media uncritically, to that same extent they reduce the gospel to being one more sales pitch among many.

- *The lethal effect of secularization*: 'Man does not live by bread alone,' Jesus said, but thanks to the brilliance and power of modern insights and techniques, no generation has come closer to the illusion of being able to do so. This illusion extends to the ability to grow churches and conduct effective outreach on the strength of human ingenuity alone. Churches grow, with very little need of God's truth or his grace. Secularism has produced, even among Christians, those who live as 'functional atheists'. The Christian mission is then driven only by statistics, demographics and the 'can-do' spirit.

- *The Midas touch of consumerism*: In a world where capitalism has produced consumerism, marketing and branding become essential. In this atmosphere, the gospel easily degenerates into just another product. At best, the result is shallow evangelism and deficient discipleship. At worst, it is unfaithfulness to the gospel. Related to this is the gospel preaching which appeals to the wrong, consumerist desires. Among the most flagrant offenders here is the 'health-and-wealth gospel', now exported from the USA and Europe to the Global South. The effects are disastrous to the gospel and cruel to the poor.

- *The idol of chronological timeliness*: In a 'fast-life' world, we care less about the past, more about our 'instant, total-information' present, and most of all about the future. But this mindset is suffused with fatal idolatries: the seductions of 'relevance', the siren call to ceaseless innovation and the appeal of unceasing novelty. The old maxim still holds true: 'He who marries the spirit of the age soon becomes a widower.'

- *Confusing or hiding the gospel*: If the gospel has sometimes been shorn of its accompanying social responsibilities, it has equally been confused by others with being only social responsibility. We cannot be vocal about injustice while being hesitant about the scandal of the cross and the saving power of Christ's substitutionary death.

- *Contributing rather than complaining*: In our globalized world which has produced shadows and injustices, not to mention fears and uncertainties, people are crying out for hope and practical solutions. Among many issues on which evangelicals have both the biblical resources and experience to speak constructively is the issue of civility in the emerging 'global public square'. Whereas some Western Christians are now widely attacked as being part of the problem of religion and public life, the proper championing of freedom of conscience and religious liberty for people of all faiths would make us part of the answer – not only for our own good, but for the wider good and the shalom of humanity. The Lausanne Movement could lead at this point.

> **We cannot be vocal about injustice while hesitant about the scandal of the cross.**

Serving God in our generation

We must face both the opportunities and the challenges of globalization as the united people of God, not simply those from this generation or that, this part of the world or that.

We must avoid the peril of two equal and opposite forms of the worldliness of power. On the one hand, we must not confuse the spread of the gospel with the spread of Western power, and on the other, we must not confuse a prophetic stand against Western power with the premises and prejudices of anti-Western 'post-colonialism'. With Western power in visible decline, there is less excuse for the first confusion than at Edinburgh, though the economic and cultural power of the West may well outlast its political and military dominance. In many parts of the world, the current temptation is to fall for the opposite confusion introduced by post-colonialism. But this would divide Christian against Christian in the name of suspicion, envy and resentment. And it would also divide the church along such lines as the West versus 'the rest', the Global North against the Global South, or the churches of the more-developed world against the churches of the less-developed world. Extra-biblical definitions and boundaries like these were the very mistake that Edinburgh 1910 made. We must not make similar mistakes today.

We all thank God together for the abundant evidence of the spectacular growth of the churches in the Global South, with all their courage, passion and spiritual power. They put to shame the all-too-obvious contrast with the spiritual poverty of churches in the West. But at the same time, we must all be humbly aware that much of the Global South is not yet fully modernized and therefore not yet fully tested by the coming challenges and seductions of modernity (to which the Western church has fallen captive). That test is still to come.

Equally, we all openly acknowledge and grieve over the dire weakness and worldliness of much of the church in the West and its profound need for revival and reformation. Yet its sorry condition can stand as a helpful warning to all the churches elsewhere in the world: do not do as Western churches have done over the past 200 years – falling captive to the spirit and systems of the modern world. Thus, all the global churches can join hands in prayer with Western churches in this hour of their greatest challenge.

Then the global churches around the whole world can be true partners and join forces to face the task of recovering a faith with such integrity and effectiveness that it can prevail over the challenges of the advanced modern world, and so do honour to our Lord and bring his good news to the world.

David F. Wells is Distinguished Senior Research Professor at Gordon Conwell Theological Seminary. www.gordonconwell.edu
(See p. 38 for Os Guinness's biographical details.)

DAY 4

PRIORITIES: Discerning the will of God for evangelization in our century

TESTIMONY: SHARING STORIES, SHARING TRUTH
Steve Evans (USA/South Africa)

Not long ago, I was in the northern part of Pakistan, in a very beautiful area, with high mountains and valleys, to lead a conference on the oral communication of God's Word. Shortly after I arrived, I met a man in his forties who owned a successful tourism business. He said, 'Before the conference starts, let's go on a hike in the mountains.' So I agreed. For half a day we walked the hills and the valleys. He was interested to know more about the conference I would be leading.

I told him we would be discussing how we could most effectively share God's Word among oral communicators in evangelism, discipleship and church planting. He asked, 'What do you mean by the work of oral communicators?' I explained that they are those who can't, won't or don't read and write.

He stopped on the trail and stared at me. 'You're talking about me,' he said. 'I'm illiterate. Even though I'm a businessman, I can't read or write. And I don't feel like I have any ministry to do for God.' But I said, 'No, that's not true. In fact, as you yourself don't read or write, I think you have advantages over many others in doing ministry for God.'

As we continued walking, a farmer called to us from the field he was hoeing. 'Come to my house for some tea,' he said. So we went and sat in his yard with his family and drank tea. Discussion centred on the mountains, the traditions of the mountains and the stories of the mountains. I said, 'You know, this discussion reminds me of a story from God's Word.'

And I began to tell them that, in the beginning, before there was anything, there was God. God spoke, and when he spoke he created everything. After I finished the story, the farmer said, 'I believe that story.' And I said, 'Yes, I believe that story too.' And I asked him, 'Would you like to hear more stories?' He said, 'Yes.' And I said, 'I'm leaving, but my friend lives here, and he will be glad to share more stories with you from God's Word.'

Before we left, I asked, 'May I pray for you and your family?' The farmer agreed. As we walked out of the yard, my new co-worker in the gospel turned to me and said, 'I didn't think it was so easy to share Bible stories.' And I said, 'Yes, it's really as easy as that.' And he said, 'I can do this.'

Steve Evans is a photojournalist, serving with the International Mission Board. He is a member of the Lausanne Orality Network. www.imb.org

EPHESIANS 4:1–16
Vaughan Roberts (UK)

John Lennon's 'Imagine' must be one of the most popular songs of the late twentieth century. Its appeal lies not just in its catchy tune, but in the compelling vision it presents. Many of us are familiar with the words:[1] Lennon asks us to imagine everyone living a life of peace, and he hopes that we will all catch the dream that the world will be as one. How we long for a world that is as one. A united world, free from the bitter hostilities that have divided humanity down the centuries. Divisions of creed and colour and class. Sometimes we make progress. The world rejoiced when the twentieth century's greatest symbol of division, the Berlin Wall, was toppled, and four years later apartheid in South Africa was dismantled. And yet, for the wise, the joy is always tinged with sadness, for progress in one place is always matched by conflict in another: between Palestinians and Israelis in the Middle East, between the Taliban and allied forces in Afghanistan, between Muslims and Christians in Sudan, in Nigeria, and many other places.

In one sense, we've never been more united. We live in a truly global society, drawn together by the internet. We watch the same television programmes; we drink the same colas. And yet we're as divided as ever. And Christians aren't surprised by that. We know that as soon as human beings push God out of the world, division always follows: we're divided from God, from creation, from one another. The low point, of course, was the tower of Babel, as God in his judgment scattered human beings to different areas, different languages. Division grieves us, but Christians will never despair, because we know that God has a cosmic, eternal plan to put everything right.

It's this great plan we've been thinking about as we've studied Ephesians: to unite all things in Christ, things in heaven and on earth (1:10). God promised Abraham that he would fulfil that plan. He said that through the seed of Abraham all nations would be blessed and brought together. And we live in the days of fulfilment. As Christ hung on the cross, he threw his arms wide so that he might draw all peoples to himself, all who through faith would trust in his sacrificial death for them. And then he sent his followers into the nations to proclaim the gospel, and by his Spirit he is drawing people to believe in Christ through the gospel. The Holy Spirit is drawing people together: to God, to one another. And the fruit of that great work of gathering by the Spirit through the gospel is being seen in more and more local churches, scattered throughout the world.

They may look so unimpressive: sometimes just a few people in a home. And yet that unimpressive local church is a pointer to the future, a foretaste of the perfect unity of everything. And so in a world of division, people should be able to look to the diverse group of Christians in any local church – different personalities, backgrounds, sometimes different races – and say, 'Wow! How those Christians love one another!' Yet often, far from being attracted by our unity, the world is repelled by the divisions both within local churches and across local churches. It's a tragedy, and it's why the theme of this great passage is so urgent. Paul proclaims two great truths:

Two requirements of Christian unity
Christian unity requires (i) an outworking of God's call; and (ii) a proclamation of God's Word.

An outworking of God's call
First, Christian unity requires an outworking of God's call. 'I therefore, a prisoner for the Lord, urge you to walk in a manner worthy of the calling to which you have been called' (verse 1). Here is the great turning point of the letter. In the light of what God has done for us in Christ, Paul says, 'Therefore here is how you are to live.' From this verse onwards, Paul spells out the implications of Christ's work in us by the Spirit. He begins with living together in unity. Unity is at the heart of God's plan, and unity must be the first thing that we are urgently to spell out and live out.

Notice (verse 3) we are not urged to *become* united. We are to be eager to *maintain* the unity of the Spirit. Christian unity is not something we can achieve; it is a fact, because of the saving work of God himself. We are one body (verse 4), because we have been called by the one God, the Father, through the one Spirit to believe in the one Lord, Jesus Christ. And although we are very different – that's obvious as we look around – we share one faith, one baptism, one hope.

Our unity is not organizational or denominational; it is spiritual. The twentieth century could be called the ecumenical century. The momentum for the Ecumenical Movement began exactly 100 years ago, at the Edinburgh Missionary Conference, as Christians gathered from around the world, with the noble aim of the evangelization of the world in their generation. Many divisions between Christian groups were not only obstacles to mission, but an affront to God, and Christians resolved to work towards visible unity. There was much that was very good and very right about that. But as time went by, a concern for unity led to a marginalization of doctrinal truth, and ecumenism drifted into what Jim Packer has called 'ecumania': 'the uncontrollable urge to merge', with its mantra 'Love unites, doctrine divides.' There has been a trend towards lowest-common-denominator theology, which has been willing to water down or even abandon core doctrines in order to keep people together.

The hand of unquestioning Christian fellowship has been offered, all in the name of unity, even to those who deny such truths as the uniqueness of Christ, and the sanctity of marriage as the only context for sexual intercourse. That is not the unity which Paul speaks of here. Unity of the Spirit is not something we can create by ecumenical effort; it's the unity that God himself has created by the gospel. It is spiritual, it is evangelical, it is unity which hasn't sidelined truth. God has used truth to bring it about. In Ephesians 1:13 Paul says, 'And you also were included in Christ when you heard the word of truth, the gospel of your salvation.' Through the truth, through the gospel, by the Spirit, we are one family in Christ with all converted people, made alive by the miraculous work of God. And now Paul calls us to live out the implications of that truth. To walk (verse 1) in a manner worthy of the calling to which you have been called.

Lindsay Brown's excellent book *Shining like Stars: The Power of the Gospel in the World's Universities* relates a moving example of living out that unity. He describes a time of great tension in Burundi between Tutsis and Hutus. A number of Hutus were killed on campus as a result of tribal fighting, so many of their fellow Hutus fled to the mountains. Their Tutsi Christian fellow-students followed them with food and clothing. Once they had seen to the needs of the Christians, they then helped the others. As a result of doing this, some Tutsis were rejected by their families, because they put the claims of Christ and their fellow Christians above allegiance to tribe and family. The non-Christian Principal of that university said this: 'Our culture is disintegrating. On our campus there are three types of people. There are Hutus, there are Tutsis and there are Christians. If our culture is to survive, we must follow the example of the Christians.'[2] It's a very challenging example. Too often we only make the effort to offer fellowship and love to Christians like us: same tribe, same race, same class, same grouping, same convictions on every minor detail. The notice outside one church said this: 'We are a pre-millennial, dispensationalist, single-rapture church and we welcome all who are one with us in Christ Jesus.' We all do it in different ways. We put up barriers and we imply that you're only really welcome if you're exactly like us. Paul says, 'No. Be eager to maintain the unity of the Spirit.'

That does not begin with commissions to discuss organizational unity (though they have their place). It does not begin with great global congresses like this (though these have a place too). But it begins with the daily battle against sin in local churches. We are called (verse 2) to live with all humility and gentleness. So often our divisions are not because of differences in theological principle, but because of pride, as we ignore those who are different, treat them as if they are beneath us, think of ourselves as so important. We strut around, expecting everyone else to fit in with our preferences. We take offence quickly; we nurse grievances. Paul says, 'No. Bear with one another in love.' It's only by the gracious love of God that we belong to his family. That gracious love is to be the model for our relationships within the local church and across all our dealings – with other churches, with other organizations. Then when we look at other people, we won't immediately think 'difference'. It's easy to do. 'Oh they're not like us. They're Arminian. They're Calvinist. They're charismatic. They're conservative. They're Baptist. They're Presbyterian.' We should rather see the born-again believer as first and foremost a *Christian*. We're brothers and sisters. We're family. As someone said, 'Love for those who are *like* us is ordinary. Love for those who are *unlike* us is extraordinary. Love for those who *dislike* us is revolutionary.' And that is the kind of love to which our Lord God calls us. Christian unity requires an outworking of God's call.

Christian unity requires a proclamation of God's Word.
Unity doesn't mean uniformity. Paul has stressed our oneness in verses 1–6, and in verse 7 he speaks of one way in which we are different. 'But,' he says, 'grace was given to each one of us according to the measure of Christ's gift.' He's speaking about the different spiritual gifts that we've all received. When human beings freeze water, we make ice cubes, all exactly the same. But when God freezes water, he makes snowflakes, every one different. And God has given us different gifts within the body. We're familiar with the body image from 1 Corinthians 12. It's here in this passage too, in verse 16. It's as the whole body, and all the different parts of the body, do their work, that the church is built up.

Paul doesn't talk here about all the different gifts Christ gives. He focuses on just a few. In verses 8–10 he describes how the Lord Jesus has ascended into heaven in fulfilment of Psalm 68, and just as the king distributes booty after a great victory, so the ascended Christ distributes gifts to his people. He gave the church the apostles, the prophets, the evangelists, the shepherds and teachers. We've seen the apostles and prophets earlier in the letter; in 2:20 we read that the church is built on the foundation of the apostles and prophets. You might think that meant New Testament apostles and Old Testament prophets, until you read 3:4, 5, where Paul speaks of the mystery of Christ which was not made known in other generations as it has now been revealed by the Spirit to God's holy apostles and prophets. The prophets and apostles here are those who first received the revelation of the gospel in the first century. We may believe in a continuing gift of prophecy today. Some believe in a continuing gift of apostleship today. But we should never equate those gifts with these foundational gifts to those who first received the revelation of the gospel. Those who regard themselves as prophets or apostles should not make over-vaunted claims today. They are not like these first-generation apostles and prophets who received the revelation of the gospel.

Then there are the evangelists, those who first proclaimed the gospel to unbelievers, and the shepherds and teachers. Notice the definite article, which comes only once, very likely referring to one group of people: those who are 'shepherds and teachers', those who shepherd by teaching. They are under-shepherds. Those of us who are pastors, never forget who the pastor of your local church is: not you, not me, but the Lord Jesus Christ, and we are under-shepherds. He exercises his shepherding of the church as we pastor the congregation through the Word of God. The ministry of the Word is vital for the church. Through the preaching of the gospel, the Holy Spirit gathers people to himself, and through the ministry of the Word, the Spirit does his work in people's lives, enabling the church to grow as it should. These Word gifts lead to a variety of different consequences.

For a start (verse 12), they lead to ministry. He gave the church the apostles, the prophets, the evangelists, the shepherds and teachers, to equip the saints for the work of ministry, for building up the body of Christ. All the flock do ministry; all the flock are ministers. I like the church that had a sign outside it: 'Pastor: Joe

Bloggs, Ministers: the whole congregation.' That's absolutely right.
So often our churches are rather like a bus. You get on the bus and
you sit passively in rows of seats. There are only two people doing
any work: one driving, and another collecting money. Isn't that
uncomfortably like many of our churches? If we are to reach the
world, if we are to build the church, then *all* the people of God need
to do their works of ministry. The ministry of those with Word gifts
functions as a kind of catalyst which equips the congregation for
their works of service. Word gifts lead to ministry of the whole
people of God.

They lead, next, to unity, (verse 13): 'until we all attain to the
unity of the faith and of the knowledge of the Son of God'. Unity
of *the* faith. It's talking about the objective truths of the gospel
expressed in propositional statements. You can't express truth any
other way. The gospel comes propositionally. Great statements like
'God is love', 'all have sinned', 'Christ died for sins' are propositional truths. But they never exist just 'out there' as propositional
truths. These truths are believed by the power of the Spirit. This
propositional truth leads to personal knowledge. This truth is
personal too. As the ministry of the Word is exercised (verse 13),
we attain to the unity of the faith and of the knowledge of the Son
of God.

I sometimes say to couples as they get married that a Christian
marriage is rather like an isosceles triangle. You've got the Lord
Jesus at the top, and the husband and wife on each of the bottom
corners. The closer they get to him, the closer they get to each other.
And a church is like a bicycle wheel. All the individuals are like
spokes, and the closer we get to the hub, which is the Lord Jesus
Christ, the closer we get to one another. And as the Word is taught,
believed and obeyed, people grow in knowledge and love of the
Lord Jesus and into unity with one another. These Word gifts are
vital for ministry, for unity.

Verse 13 continues, 'until we all attain to the unity of the faith
and of the knowledge of the Son of God, to mature manhood, to
the measure of the stature of the fullness of Christ, so that we may

no longer be children, tossed to and fro by the waves and carried about by every wind of doctrine, by human cunning, by craftiness in deceitful schemes'. Many of our churches are childish. There's a famine of the Word of God in our world. There's no greater problem than that, and we need to pray that the Lord would send out evangelists. But the tragedy is not only that there's this famine in the world, but that there's a famine of the Word of God in our churches. So we can see great growth, many people coming to Christ, but so little teaching. The great work of discipleship through the Word of God which is so keenly needed is missing. It's been called the 'great omission'. No wonder many of our churches are unstable; they've got no discernment. They're tossed like a small boat on a raging sea by every wind of doctrine that blows through. And what's the antidote? 'Rather, speaking the truth in love, we are to grow up in every way into him who is the head, into Christ.' We're to speak the truth in love (verse 15). That's the task of the evangelist, the task of the pastor-teacher, and as the pastor-teachers speak the truth in love, it's the task of the whole people of God so that our churches can be filled with the Word of God. Through preaching, pastoring, one-to-one Bible study: in all ways we need to be urging people to live in the light of the gospel.

> **There's a famine of the Word of God in our churches.**

Truth and love. We need both. Truth is not a weapon to be used to attack anyone who does not agree with us on every little detail. Some people enjoy a theological fight much too much. We must love one another. But we must also be committed to truth. Love demands truth-telling. And so evangelists, pastor-teachers, these gifts of the ministry of the Word of God are absolutely central in God's plan to bring all things together in Christ. As the Word of God goes out, people come to Christ, people from all nations are brought together in Christ. As people hear, believe and obey it, we grow to maturity in Christ. As we all exercise our ministry, we grow into a deeper maturity in Christ.

God's will for evangelism

There's no greater need in world mission than the recruiting, training, deploying of a whole new generation of those who will minister the Word of God, in his world and in his church. And we should commit ourselves (i) to the task of recruiting, pleading with the Lord of the harvest to send out labourers into his harvest field; (ii) to pray for the risen and ascended Christ to give these gifts to his church; and (iii) to discern, recognize and encourage those who have them.

We are to invest resources in training evangelists and pastor-teachers. So much of our training is weak, and the emphasis is not on the ministry of the Word of God as it should be. We are to invest in the colleges, the extension programmes, the internships, not just to fill the gaps in our denominations, but to reach the world. Recruit, train, deploy *and maintain*. The tragedy is that many who have been recruited and trained and deployed for Word ministry are distracted into other things and do not make this main thing *the* main thing.

The book of Acts is really the story of the progress of the Word throughout the world by the Spirit, and as the Word goes out, there are great obstacles as Satan fires his darts. One of the greatest challenges comes in Acts 6. It looks so innocent. There's a squabble going on between different widows about the distribution of care for the poor. Yet that little squabble is a great danger, because it could distract the apostles from the ministry entrusted to them, the ministry of the Word and prayer. They did not say, 'Oh forget the widows; practical things don't matter. We're just concerned with spiritual priorities.' They made provision for practical needs, and so should we. But they appointed others, the deacons, to fulfil that task. Luke says, 'So the word of God spread' (Acts 6:7), and the task of global evangelization continued as Satan's great ploy had not worked.

But tragically, it has worked in many, many places, as evangelists, pastors and teachers are deflected from the ministry of the Word and prayer, as they commit themselves to the latest ministerial fashion. They are like ships on the sea, blown from one thing to the next, rather than giving themselves for the next twenty, thirty, forty years to the ministry of the Word and prayer. It looks like unglamorous, discouraging work. But this is the great ministry of reconciliation by which God brings people to Christ and matures people in Christ. And as the Word of God goes out by the Spirit, we will find our churches growing, our unity deepening, and more and more people will say, 'Look how those Christians love one another.' And they will have a foretaste of the great unity of all things that will one day be seen when God is all in all, with Christ bringing everything together in him, and then at last the world will truly be as one.

Vaughan Roberts is Rector of St Ebbe's Church, Oxford, UK, and President of the Proclamation Trust. www.stebbes.org.uk www.proctrust.org.uk

WHAT IS GOD'S GLOBAL URBAN MISSION?
Tim Keller (USA)

I'm going to look at why we must reach the great megacities of the world for Christ, how we should reach them, and why we can.

Cities: important culturally, missiologically and viscerally

Culturally

The *Financial Times* and *Foreign Policy*, significant international journals, both produced major issues on the importance of megacities in 2010.[3] In *Foreign Policy*, we read:

> The 21st century will not be dominated by America or China, Brazil or India, but by the city. In an age that appears increasingly unmanageable, cities rather than states are becoming the islands of governance on which the future world order will be built . . . Time, technology, and population growth have massively accelerated the advent of this new urbanized era. Already, more than half the world lives in cities, and the percentage is growing rapidly. Just 100 cities account for 30% of the world's economy, and almost all its innovation.[4]

If we want human life as it is lived in this world to be shaped by Jesus Christ, we have to go to the city.

Missiologically

Let's look at four kinds of people:

(i) *Young adults*, disproportionately, want to live in cities. That's where they go, and you've got to go to where they are. If you want to reach the new generation, in whatever culture, you've got to go to cities.

(ii) The *most unreached peoples* in the world are more reachable in cities. When they migrate, from rural areas in their homeland or to other countries' cities, they break kinship ties and, in a more pluralistic environment, they're far more open to the gospel, humanly speaking, than they would ever have been in their previous habitat. If you want to reach the most unreached peoples in the world, go to cities.

(iii) *Those who make films, write books and do business deals* are in the cities. Such individuals are those who have the biggest impact on our culture.

(iv) Lastly, *the poor* are in cities. One third of all people moving into the great cities of the world are going to live in shanty towns. And God cares about the poor. He loves the poor.

Viscerally

By this I mean 'from the heart'. Jonah is unhappy because God has not destroyed the great city of Nineveh (Jonah 4). But he's very happy with the vine that has grown up to protect him. It's a beautiful vine, and he's become emotionally attached to it because it's beautiful and it gives him shelter in that hot environment. It's natural and right to love part of God's green earth. But when the vine dies, he gets anguished, discouraged and depressed. And God makes an argument. God says to him, 'You were emotionally attached to the vine and not caring about what happens to Nineveh. Jonah, you love plants. But I love people.'

Psalm 19 tells us that nature reflects God's glory. But human beings, according to Genesis 1, are made in the image of God and reflect God's glory more than anything else in creation. In cities you have more image of God per square inch than anywhere else in the world. So God makes a numbers argument: 'Jonah, there are 120,000 people in Nineveh who do not know their right hand from their left.' (This was a massive number for the time.) 'How can you not be moved by that?'

A missionary friend of mine once quipped, 'The country is where there are more plants than people, and the city is where there are more people than plants. Because God loves people more than plants, he's got to love the city more than the country.' That is exactly God's argument to Jonah. People are streaming into the city. Three hundred years ago, fewer than 3% of the world's population lived in cities. Today, it's over 50% and growing rapidly. Some 8 million people, every two months, move into the cities of the world.[5] That's one new Bangkok every two months. If you love what God loves (that's the visceral), you'll love the city. If you want to go where the people are going, you've got to go to the city. And our churches are not going to the city nearly as fast as the people are. That's why we must reach the city.

> **Because God loves people more than plants, he's got to love the city more than the country.**

How then should we reach the city?

Urban China is different from China, urban America different from America, urban Africa different from Africa. When you take churches that have been forged in a rural context and place a mirror model in an urban context, they're not effective, and we wonder why. Churches have to be contextualized for the city. Let's look at this under six headings.

First, churches in the city have to be very patient in matters of cultural sensitivity, for they will always have people from different cultures. Every culture conceives differently of time, of emotional expressiveness, of honour and shame and of decision-making. An effective city-centre church in these great global cities will be multi-cultural. You always have to be patient, listening to charges of cultural insensitivity and knowing you'll never get everything right. The fact that you are open, learning and patient proves you have begun to contextualize for a city.

Secondly, city churches have to show how faith relates to work, jobs and vocation. For people in cities, work plays a much bigger part in their lives than it does for those outside of cities. And as Dorothy Sayers, the British essayist said, 'How can anyone remain interested in a religion which seems to have no concern with nine-tenths of his life?'[6] For urban dwellers, nine-tenths of life is work.

I remember an actor who had just become a Christian at my church, asking me to disciple him. He asked, 'What roles should I take as a Christian, and what roles should I not take?' Then he said, 'What do you think of method acting?'

I asked, 'What's method acting?'

He explained, 'Here, in America, they say, "Don't act angry, get angry." But in Britain, they say, "Act angry." Which should it be? What does the Christian faith have to say in response to such things?'

I looked at him and said, 'I have no idea.' The only way I knew how to disciple people was by bringing them out of their work-world and into my church-world. This was what I had been taught in seminary. But if you're in an urban church, you can't do that. You have to help people integrate their faith with their work. It could equally have been a question from a banker or a medic.

Thirdly, you have to be constantly open to disorder and change. You have to be able to live with them, and know you're going to live with them.

Fourthly, your church has to be both intensely evangelistic and famous for its concern for justice. You can't afford not to have that balance if you're an urban church.

Fifthly, there has to be a commitment to the arts. Churches outside the city do not usually need to be as attentive to the arts. But in the city you have to be.

Sixthly, churches in the city have to cooperate with churches of other denominations and traditions. Elsewhere, you can afford not to, and live and work in your own tribe. We'll never reach the city unless we collaborate with believers across denominational lines.

We need to equip church members to live out Christian values in the public arenas. City-wide affinity groups can be particularly effective. Here iron can sharpen iron, and those who are older and more senior can act as mentors to those who are younger.

TRUTH AND THE PUBLIC ARENAS

The interlocking arenas of government, business and academia have a strong influence on the values of each nation, and in human terms define the freedom of the church.

a. We encourage Christ-followers to be actively engaged in these spheres, both in public service or private enterprise, in order to shape societal values and influence public debate. We encourage support for Christ-centred schools and universities that are committed to academic excellence and biblical truth.

b. Corruption is condemned in the Bible. It undermines economic development, distorts fair decision-making and destroys social cohesion. No nation is free of corruption. We invite Christians in the workplace, especially young entrepreneurs, to think creatively about how they can best stand against this scourge.[7]

c. We encourage young Christian academics to consider a long-term career in the secular university, to (i) teach and (ii) develop their discipline from a biblical worldview, thereby to influence their subject field. We dare not neglect the academy.[8]

The Cape Town Commitment IIA7

Abraham's prayer for the city

Many of us are defeatist, afraid of the big cities; we don't know how to reach them. But we can do it.

In Genesis 18, God visits Abraham and says, 'I'm going to your neighbouring cities of Sodom and Gomorrah, and I'm going to destroy them.' Let us not miss Abraham's remarkable response to God. *First*, he begins to pray for an unbelieving city. That's unique in the Old Testament. Moses, Samuel and Jeremiah prayed for their own people, but Abraham begins to pray for these unbelieving cities. You may say he was concerned about his nephew Lot who lived there. But why didn't Abraham say, 'Get Lot free, then blast them'? Instead, he prays for unbelieving, wicked pagans in these cities.

In doing so, he endangers himself for their sake, in approaching God – the Holy God – asking him again and again to spare the city. Abraham knows how dangerous this is, and at one point he says, 'I, who am but dust and ashes, let me speak again.' If spared, Sodom and Gomorrah would continue to be a threat to Abraham. This could have been his opportunity to get rid of them. But he risked his life for them. Notice his theological case. He says, 'If there are fifty righteous men, or forty, or thirty, will you spare this city, which deserves destruction?' Abraham was acting as a representative, a high priest. He was saying, is it possible that the righteousness of the few could secure mercy for the many, and somehow save them?

In the end, Sodom and Gomorrah were destroyed. They didn't have the high priest they needed, but we do. Jesus Christ is the ultimate High Priest. Abraham prayed for people, interceded for people who might have killed him. But Jesus Christ said, 'Father, forgive them! They don't know what they're doing.' Jesus Christ interceded for people who *did* kill him. Abraham risked his life for these unbelieving cities, but Jesus *gave* his life for unbelievers. Abraham had a theological concept: 'Isn't it possible that somehow the righteousness of the few might cover the sin of the many?' But Jesus Christ is the reality. Jesus Christ is the only righteous one who could do it: 'God made him who had no sin to be sin for us, so that in him we might become the righteousness of God' (2 Corinthians 5:21).

Jesus Christ is the reality to which Abraham pointed. And when we find him as our Saviour, when he becomes our High Priest, we become the priests that the cities of this world need. We can pray for them like the Jews were told, 'Pray for Babylon and seek the peace of the city' (Jeremiah 29:7). We should lay down our lives for the people in the city. They should see that we care about them, that we love them, as our neighbours. We should pray for them, because we have been empowered to be the priests the cities need. Most of all, we should offer the righteousness of Jesus Christ to cover their sin, that they may be saved.

'Look at the cities of this world. Look at the masses of these cities,' God tells us. 'Why aren't you moved by them? Why aren't you going there?' So let's go!

Tim Keller is founder and pastor of New York's Redeemer Presbyterian Church in Manhattan, and a New York Times *best-selling author.*
www.redeemer.com www.redeemercitytocity.com

ETHICS, EMERGING TECHNOLOGIES AND THE HUMAN FUTURE
Nigel Cameron (UK/USA) and John Wyatt (UK)

What does it mean to be human? In traditional thought, there has always been a clear distinction between 'natural' beings, derived from the natural order, and those that were 'artefacts', a product of human ingenuity and craft. For many centuries, our embodied human nature was the last frontier of the natural order. Although human beings could modify every other aspect of their environment, they could not escape the 'given-ness' of their own humanity.

But the rapid development of emerging technologies is about to create a new and profoundly troubling assault on human identity. This cuts to the quick of our anthropology: it focuses on the fundamental relationship between our artefacts and our own nature, our manipulative capabilities and our own selves. It was this recognition that drove C. S. Lewis, back in 1943, to write his prophetic essay, 'The Abolition of Man', perhaps the most penetrating statement yet made of the greatest question that will confront the 'biotech century'. The significance of our belief that we are made in the image of God is about to be tested as never before.

Lewis argued that, while technology *appeared* to extend the human race's ability to control and subdue nature,

> . . . what we call Man's power over Nature turns out to be a power exercised by some men over other men with Nature as its instrument . . . Each new power won by Man is a power over Man. Each advance leaves him weaker as well as stronger. In every victory, besides the general who triumphs, is a prisoner who follows the triumphal car. Human nature will be the last part of Nature to surrender to Man. We shall be henceforth free to make our species whatever we wish it to be. The battle will indeed be won. But who, precisely, will have won it? Man's final conquest has proved to be the abolition of Man.

In other words, by taking to ourselves the power to determine our own future, we turn ourselves into creatures of our own design, artefacts of our own manufacture.

Human dignity and the 'biotech century'

The question we face is what to do with the extraordinary new powers that we are taking to ourselves. Developments in human genetics, biotechnology, pharmacology, neuroscience and nano-medicine raise high hopes of cures for terrible diseases, including inherited disorders, cancer and degenerative conditions. Yet as C. S. Lewis warned, the spectacular promise which these technologies offer, driven in part by a noble desire to combat the destructive consequences of disease, always carries a darker side – the manipulation of vulnerable human lives.

We are gaining unparalleled understanding of the human genome, and this new knowledge could lead to precisely targeted drugs and sophisticated new clinical applications. But the explosion in genetic knowledge has also led directly to new and sophisticated means of identifying and destroying embryonic and foetal human beings who carry unwanted genetic variants. This way of dealing with disease, by destroying those who carry it, offends the consciences of many more than those who call themselves 'pro-life'. It should perhaps be no surprise that in Germany, where they have not forgotten what eugenics means, *in-vitro* fertilization is perfectly legal, but embryos must be implanted without quality control.

Reproductive technology has enabled couples to overcome the pain of infertility, but it has also led to the deliberate creation of embryonic human beings for destructive research, and the creation of cloned embryos and even human-animal hybrids. As Oliver O'Donovan warned, we have replaced 'the old-fashioned crime of killing babies' with 'the new and subtle crime of making babies to be ambiguously human, of presenting to us members of our own species who are doubtfully proper objects of compassion and love'.

There is a tendency for ethically conservative religious people to define such debates solely in 'pro-life' terms. This does not help their cause with those in the science, business and policy communities who are resistant to calls for ethical limitations in these technologies. By asserting their position on abortion as the paradigm of the agenda, they unwittingly marginalize themselves, and make it difficult to build common cause with wider forces in the culture – who may share many of their concerns about particular aspects of the technologies in question, about the need in principle for limits, and about the profound significance of these questions of policy.

We make a big mistake if we see discussion of the human future as mainly concerning reproductive and embryo issues, for the most sobering scenarios lie ahead and elsewhere. In the field of neuro-science, the emerging technologies are enabling us to monitor, control, manipulate and enhance our brain function. It is becoming increasingly possible to manipulate perception and memory, whether through neuro-pharmacology (including what has been termed 'cosmetic neurology') or cognitive prostheses.

The goal of technology is not only to understand the world, but to control it, and neuroscience offers potent new possibilities for social control. Take all the forms of human behaviour which threaten our future – violence, inter-racial conflict, religious fanaticism, addiction, the selfish squandering of the world's resources. At heart, these can all be seen as due to the malfunctioning of the human brain. If we can only understand how to prevent this faulty cognitive processing, we will be able to usher in a new dawn of social harmony and global peace. By making our own human functioning an object of scientific study – by objectifying ourselves – we hope to control ourselves, to achieve self-mastery.

Since so-called 'religious fundamentalism' is regarded as a major source of social and political conflict, it is not surprising that an active area of neuroscience research is into the brain mechanisms which underlie religious beliefs and experiences, and the cognitive processes which lie at the formation of moral beliefs and the resolution of moral conflicts and dilemmas. It does not require much imagination to see the manipulative and coercive possibilities which this knowledge will bring. At the same time, advances in stem-cell technology and regenerative medicine enable us to enhance our functioning and extend human life-span, and create human-machine interfaces of unparalleled power.

Genetic and biological science erodes the traditional distinction between humanity and the animal world. We are merely one primate species among many others. On the other hand, emerging technologies erode the distinction between the human and the artefact. We are merely machines made out of carbon instead of silicon. How can we preserve our unique human identity and help to create a genuinely pro-human future in the light of these technological challenges?

God's perspective

As biblical Christians, our starting point remains in the creation narratives of Genesis, where we read that humans are made in the image of God himself, with a mandate to rule and steward the creation for God, and in the New Testament, where we read that Jesus Christ is God made flesh, God himself taking our human form. So Christians are called to treat the human body, with its strange and idiosyncratic design, with special respect. This is the form in which God became flesh. We are neither animals nor machines – we are humans made in God's image; he has taken that image for his own by becoming one of us in our membership of the species *Homo sapiens*. As we rule and steward the creation, including the extraordinary possibilities of science and technology, it is as human beings accountable and responsible to him, and stewards of what he has made.

The 'pro-human' cause presents itself as the great question of our century, as we confront the rapid development of emerging technologies and their offer of powers to aid or undermine our humanness at the most fundamental level.

Key questions raised by emerging technologies

Several sets of questions should be on our minds as we consider policy approaches to these technologies. A future that is both pro-technology and pro-human will depend on their answers.

1. *Commodification*. As our powers extend over our own bodies and the bodies of others, and technologies lead to products and processes, questions of intellectual property will occupy centre-stage. A case in point: in the United States there was a recent debate over whether human embryos could be patented. The biotechnology industry, through its trade group BIO, argued that genetically engineered human embryos were appropriate subjects of patent claims. How can we protect vulnerable human beings – the modern equivalents of widows, orphans and aliens – from the manipulative possibilities of technology?

2. *Eugenics*. There is growing pressure for eugenic uses of *in-vitro* fertilization, not simply to screen out embryos with genetic diseases, but to select the sex and other 'desirable' inherited characteristics of our future children. And within society, there is corresponding pressure for various forms of genetic discrimination, in employment and insurance especially. In Christian thought, the dignity of a human being resides not in our function or our biological potential, but in what we are, by creation. In the literal words of the eighth Psalm, each one of us is 'lacking a very little of God' (Psalm 8:5). Our human dignity is *intrinsic*, in the way we have been made, in how God remembers us and calls us. How can we preserve and defend the biblical understanding that each human life has a unique and incalculable value because of the indwelling image of God?

3. *'Enhancement'*. Whether through genetics or nanotechnology and cybernetics, it is likely that we shall see human enhancements developed, especially in cognition, in effect blending human and machine through such means as the implanting of brain chips for memory, skills or communication. The logic of such developments is far-reaching, since while they would begin incrementally and through dual-use devices with genuine medical applications (for example, for stroke victims), and they would have a longer-term impact through compounding both the intelligence and the wealth of a small segment of society, perhaps leading ultimately to a new feudalism in which power of all kinds is concentrated in the hands of 'enhanced' persons.

We should also note the steady growth of 'transhumanism', a network of science-fiction enthusiasts and outlandish thinkers who deliberately seek radical changes in human nature. They have recently begun to move from the fringes of society into mainstream contexts, and are pressing the idea of radical 'enhancement' in academic and policy-making circles.

God's priority for humanity

In contrast, the resurrection of Christ as a physical human being can be seen as God's vote of confidence in the created human nature. The original design of human beings is not abandoned, despised or marginalized; it is affirmed and fulfilled. In Jesus, the second Adam, we see both a perfect human being – what the original Adam was meant to be – and we see the pioneer, the blueprint for a new type of person – the one in whose likeness a new creation will spring, the first-fruits of those who are to come (1 Corinthians 15:20). God declares that for all future time he will sustain, redeem and transform the humanity that was originally made.

The resurrection is God's final and irrevocable 'yes' to humankind. If we take the biblical doctrines of the incarnation and resurrection seriously, perhaps we should conclude that the physical structure of our human bodies is not something we are free to change without very careful thought. How can emerging technologies with their extraordinary power be used not to manipulate and destroy, but to better fulfil our humanness?

Conclusion

The great issues of ethics and policy that we face are all focused on questions of human dignity and the significance of human nature.

Developments in emerging technologies are leading to very great increases in our power over human nature itself. At the heart of the agenda for the twenty-first century lies the need to build a policy framework, in which ethical principles set the ground rules for our use of these new powers. In parallel with legislative and regulatory interventions in the technology arena, (i) the intellectual property landscape must be shaped to secure human nature from com-moditization, and (ii) genetic discrimination, itself the obverse of eugenics, must be comprehensively outlawed.

A robust approach to each of these questions will enable us to welcome emerging technologies. They have extraordinary capacity to enhance, not human nature, but our capacity to be human, that we may better fulfil our humanness. At the same time (as our recent experience of genetically modified foods demon-strates), it is not in the interests of the scientific or business communities to develop technologies that are freighted with controversy. Christians who would take a lead in the development of pro-human technology policies will find allies in many quarters.

The great issues of ethics are all focused on the significance of human nature.

Of course, every application of every new technology will be presented to us as yet another wonderful benefit for human beings that will make life better and easier. The brave-new-world ques-tion that must always be asked is: at what cost? Lewis's essay on 'The Abolition of Man' opens with a potent quotation from John Bunyan's *Pilgrim's Progress*, with which we conclude: 'It came burning hot into my mind, whatever he said and however he flattered, when he got me home to his house, he would sell me for a slave.'

Nigel Cameron is President and CEO of the Center for Policy on Emerging Technologies in Washington DC, and Chairman of BioCentre in London. John Wyatt is Emeritus Professor of Neonatal Paediatrics at University College, London, and a board member of BioCentre.
www.c-pet.org www.bioethics.ac.uk www.ucl.ac.uk

DAY 5

INTEGRITY: Calling the church of Christ back to humility, integrity and simplicity

TESTIMONY: SHAKING SALT, SHINING LIGHT IN NATIONAL LIFE
Paul Batchelor (UK)

Recently I was in Zambia with members of my family. During our stay we visited three schools. None was well equipped, and the walls were mostly bare. In each school, two pieces of information were painted on the walls to attract the attention of pupils. One was a warning about HIV/AIDS, with a simple definition of what it is, and an explanation of how to avoid it. The second was a warning about corruption, and some of the consequences were carefully laid out. Having spent a significant part of my working life in Africa, I was not shocked to see such warnings on classroom walls.

Much of our host continent, so rich in natural resources, and in Christian joy, has been massively afflicted by corruption over the past fifty years. Of course, corrupt practice existed long before then; the colonial record is far from unblemished. But its scale and effects have grown hugely. The great optimism that hailed independence in the 1960s, when I first worked here as a volunteer, has all too often given way to dismay and anger, as efforts to promote economic and social development have been systematically undermined. This has left a tiny minority with untold, ill-gotten wealth, while the great majority of people still endure grinding poverty. For many of our African brothers and sisters, the reality and painful effects of corruption are everyday facts of life. Some, whether Christians or not, get caught up in it; some boldly try to resist it; but none can simply ignore it. No wonder the issue is high on the agenda of schools.

The same can be said of large parts of South Asia and Latin America and parts of South East Asia and Eastern Europe. Here, too, people face a daily struggle against the impact of corruption, and some courageously stand against it.

By contrast, many of us in more affluent parts of the world indulge in the mistaken belief that corruption does not really affect us. Yet if we open our newspapers, the facts are plain. In the UK, for example, we read of scandals such as the dishonest expenses claims by Members of Parliament, or allegations of match-fixing, or obscenely high levels of pay for a privileged few, or corporate bribery. If matters do not actually impinge on our daily lives or threaten our survival, somehow we persuade ourselves that they do not, or need not, concern us. We can feel complacent or arrogant and 'pass by on the other side', thankful perhaps that 'we are not as those others are' who indulge in such things.

This mistaken sense of its not being our problem may be why, in an internet search on phrases like 'Christians combatting corruption', most entries relate to Africa, and Nigeria, Kenya and Uganda feature prominently. In those countries, people feel the effects of corruption acutely every day.

Corruption crosses ethnic, class and faith boundaries. Christians are not immune, and some churches have succumbed to corrupt practices. But there are also many good stories to tell, not least from Africa. African Christians in positions of influence have become actively engaged in the struggle to arrest corruption's blight, and have set us a great example. The time has come to make this a truly global effort among evangelicals, for corruption is not just a localized phenomenon. And it is not a victimless crime: its impact on people, on whole nations, and on the work of the church — both in evangelism and social action — can be extremely damaging.

The Bible offers clear teaching on the causes and consequences of corruption, and on the godly alternatives we are called to adopt. As the people of God, let us build ourselves up, and build one another up in Scripture's rich teaching. Let us continue to use the Bible's teaching with all wisdom, as we take forward the great endeavours of evangelical agencies. Furthermore, as Christians in the public arenas, let us use it to inform, and to reinforce, the growing secular efforts to combat corruption.

Paul Batchelor is Chairman of Crown Agents, and serves on the International Advisory Board of Transparency International.
www.crownagents.com www.transparency.org

His paper for the Government, Business and Academia think tank, co-written with Steve Osei-Mensah, may be found at www.lausanne.org

EPHESIANS 4:17 – 6:9
Calisto Odede (Kenya)

The Welsh heard the gospel and they sang about it;
The English heard the gospel and they preached it;
The Irish heard the gospel and they fought about it.

Let's extend this and include other communities:

The Americans heard the gospel and they wrote about it;
The Asians heard the gospel and they reflected and meditated
    on it;
The Hispanics heard the gospel and they celebrated it;
The Africans heard the gospel and they danced about it.

We also know sections of the church who heard the gospel and turned it into big business. As we look around the world, some of us focus on defending the gospel, some of us sing about it, others debate it – and indeed some do make business out of it.

There was a time when evangelicals were regarded as custodians of the gospel, but with shifting trends, even that word 'evangelical' needs a redefinition today. Evangelicals (and I speak as one) are being viewed more and more as people who have a fortress mentality, barricading themselves for fear of contamination by the world. We are viewed in some circles as not really engaged in missional issues, so a new term is emerging: 'post-evangelical'.

The distinction seems to lie in how far we go in engaging with societal trends. Do we view the world as an enemy or as an opportunity? The traditional three enemies of the Christian faith – the world, the flesh and the devil – are slowly being absorbed into the church, or is it that the church is being absorbed into their arena?

The distinction between Christian and non-Christian lifestyles is disappearing. Civil liberty groups lecture Christians on being tolerant, accommodating and politically correct, and we seem to have decided to cooperate fully!

Chuck Colson wrote two decades ago:

> Privately-practised religion is, I suppose, still acceptable here. But come out of your prayer closet and voice an opinion informed by religious values, and representatives from the liberal élite in our nation [referring to America] – educators, media moguls, attorneys, politicians, civil liberty groups – will have you for lunch.[1]

We seem to be losing ground, but not because we don't have the right kind of doctrines, or because we don't publish enough books, or don't have the latest model or fad or craze. We have made Christianity unpalatable by how we conduct ourselves – how we walk.

When there is no distinction between Christian and non-Christian in terms of corruption, or rates of divorce, or unmarried pregnancies, or terminated pregnancies; or in the way we lapse into traditional quasi-religious practices; or in our attitudes towards those of a different race or ethnic community, then we need to ask ourselves whether Christianity makes any difference at all.

We continue to be fascinated by new fads, ideas and models of evangelizing the world: 'How to make your church grow in three months', 'Seven ways to bulge your spiritual muscle', and so on. If you are not an adherent of the latest fad, or if you don't use the catchy phrase in vogue, you are made to feel as if you are missing your purpose in life. Yet, like the Epicurean and Stoic philosophers, some of us keep running after new ideas. Perhaps we keep looking for the next conference to attend. If we attend every conference, when do we ever sit down to implement what we've learnt? Maybe someone needs to call our bluff – that we are not the people we want others to believe we are.

In the earlier chapters of Ephesians, Paul paints a picture of our position in Christ. He has taken the Christian faith which, like a glittering diamond, he has slowly turned around for readers to see each of its many facets. He takes us on a journey all the way to heaven where we are seated with Christ, and he brings us down to earth, to the reality of living out our Christian faith.

Now he turns to us, as if to say, 'Turn the:

- orthodoxy into orthopraxy
- principles into practice
- theology into lifestyle
- position into daily living.'

How do you walk?
To do this, he uses the common language of a journey: walking. When a child takes her first step, the new parents pick up the phone and dial Grandma, excitedly screaming, 'She's walking! She's walking!' The rest of us think, 'So what? People are walking all the time.' To see new Christians learning to walk in a new way is a very moving experience, like parents watching their child. We have already seen incidences where Paul has made reference to this idea:

- 'trespasses and sins in which you once walked' (2:1–2)
- 'created in Christ Jesus for good works, which God prepared beforehand, that we should walk in them' (2:10)
- 'walk in a manner worthy of the calling to which you have been called' (4:1)
- 'that you must no longer walk as the Gentiles do' (4:17)
- 'And walk in love, as Christ loved us and gave himself up for us' (5:2)
- 'Walk as children of light' (5:8)
- 'Look carefully then how you walk, not as unwise but as wise' (5:15)

No wonder the great Chinese Christian leader, Watchman Nee, used to refer to the book of Ephesians as: 'Sit, walk and stand'.

The Maasai Moran could draw conclusions from footprints. They would know whether the footprint was that of an adult or a child;

a man or a woman; carrying a load or not; faltering or walking steadily; the direction in which they were travelling; the time since they had passed. Footprints would tell a whole story.

What does your walk reveal? What story would your walk have told if we had followed you over the last few months? What if we followed you in the week ahead, at home, in your office, in your ministry? Paul teaches us how we should walk.

1. Walk as you have learnt (Ephesians 4:17–32)

a. Not as the Gentiles

Paul starts this section by pointing out a negative to bring out a positive. The Ephesian believers are urged not to walk like the 'other Gentiles' or, as some versions would put it, like the 'heathens' or the 'pagans'. The fact that he is talking of 'other Gentiles' implies that the people he was addressing were also Gentiles, or Christians living in a mainly Gentile area.

Paul is referring either to their former lifestyles or to the fact that, since now they are converted, they do not need to live like the heathens around them. So how were the Gentiles living?

   i. In the futility of their minds
  ii. Under a cloud of darkness that seemed to have engulfed them, resulting from the hardness of their hearts. This made them alienated from God. The Ephesians are urged not to live as practical atheists who find God irrelevant.
 iii. With a 'heart' condition that led to a natural outflow of certain behaviour:
- They became callous
- They gave themselves over to sensuality
- They practised every kind of impurity, as if there was no law to live by
- They were filled with greediness and lustful corruption

This type of life should not be the trademark of believers.

b. As you've been taught in Christ

They had 'learnt Christ' in a certain way. Since they had been taught Christ's teaching, they should live their lives in the way they had been taught. Indeed, their lifestyles should be the opposite of what they had noticed among the Gentiles:

- Instead of falsehood, they should speak the truth
- Instead of being controlled by anger, they should manage it or it will lead them into sin
- Instead of stealing, they should work with their own hands to give to those who do not have
- Instead of unwholesome talk, they should speak words which edify

c. In newness of life

Paul indicated to them that they had newness of life, and so should put away all that was associated with their former lives. This includes bitterness, wrath, anger, slander and malice. Instead, they should put on forgiveness, kindness, tenderness. That kind of lifestyle will not grieve the Spirit of God who is in them. As the Kikuyu saying goes: 'Utatigaga Ndakoraga' – one who does not leave does not find. If we are to abide in the wealth and the riches of the newness of this life, we must abandon the former life.

d. Reflections

It is true that Christianity has struggled with a credibility gap recently.

    i. Some have substituted the true preaching of the gospel of the Lord Jesus Christ with pep talks on motivation and the like. How people are living no longer seems a major issue, provided they make the dollars, climb the economic ladder and enjoy the feel-good factor.

   ii. Some have regressed into a mixture of Christianity and traditional religious practices which border on the occult.

This leads people to syncretistic lifestyles where they easily relapse into pagan practices without a blink.

iii. Some ministers have become con artists who will sell you a bottle of fake oil. These men are driven more by profit and gain than by a desire for the true prophetic transformation of lives.

The true cry of the heart is for an authentic walk with the Lord. Otherwise, we will be viewed as a bunch of noisy vuvuzela-blowers standing on the periphery, and not engaging in true action where real transformation takes place.

We lose our cutting edge when people no longer see a difference between us as Christians and those of other faiths or none. The onus is on us to rise against the trends of our cultural practices, which are contrary to the Word of God and diminish our impact. We need to be different, for indeed we *are* different:

- We believe in Jesus
- We are seated in heavenly places in Christ Jesus
- We are no longer aliens, but the children of God
- We are new creations
- We live a life of fullness in the Spirit

This is an invitation to bring Christianity out of the closet, into the public arena; out of the convention halls, into the streets and market place of our cities; out of the ivory towers of theological reflections and nit-picking, into the living room and the rural market place. This is where the rubber meets the road, where the goat is turned to grass.

The missionary martyr, Jim Elliot, recorded in his journal:

I sought God in the common place,
And I found him every day,
Not in the streets of Jerusalem
Nor caressed by Galilee's spray;

But I found God on the sidewalks,
The backyard, and our upstairs,
And I walked with him on Main Street;
He handled my school affairs.

My Christ stands not in a synagogue
With a beard and a long white gown,
But I know him in the grocery store,
He rides our car downtown.
Many smile when I tell them,
Some say it is not right
To find the Lord on Broadway
'Neath the glow of a neon light.[2]

Our call is to walk with Christ in the 'everydayness' of life.

2. Walk in love (Ephesians 5:1–6)

a. Imitating God (5:1)

Paul gives the Ephesian believers a tall order: imitate God. They need to do this, as they are his beloved children. Children will imitate their parents as role models. The Ephesians are asked to make God their role model. We could say, 'Like Father, like son'.

We have God's nature in us, so we should allow him to live his life through us, and not perpetuate behaviour and habits that are not befitting for the children of God.

b. In sacrificial manner (5:2)

Paul quickly adds that the walk he desires of the Ephesians is sacrificial, as Christ's was. Christ loved us to the extent of offering up his life to God as a sacrifice. This is not cheap love, but very costly love. We have to be ready to pay the ultimate price. We are called to the road less travelled. Recently I heard the comment: 'Our pastor does not love us – he loves our money!' What an indictment! Unless we are willing to show the world a love that is costly, we will not touch it and bring transformation. While Christians are too busy competing with the Joneses, Kamaus and Patels in the rat race, sacrifice will be far from our vocabulary.

Many are labouring in very difficult and trying circumstances, making real sacrifices in their corner of the vineyard. God bless you, sir. God bless you, madam. May God help all of us not to reach out to the world with a long wooden spoon, but to feel people's pain and touch lives where it matters. As that early African church leader, Tertullian, once said, 'The blood of the martyrs is the seed of the church.'

c. Not in counterfeit love (5:3–6)

Paul follows the discussions on sacrificial love with a lengthy discourse on abstaining from every manner of sexual immorality and impurity. In a pagan environment filled with fertility cults, where people sometimes engaged with temple prostitutes, Paul's advice went strongly against the practice of the day.

The world has always offered counterfeit love in the form of sexual immorality. Our days are no different, with the movie industry churning out versions of love, and the internet spewing out its own variety of 'erotomania'. The believer who wants to walk the straight and narrow road is caught between faithfulness and compromise. Statistics show that there is no significant difference in sexual conduct or behaviour between college-age Christians and their non-Christian counterparts. In some instances, as many as 20% of those who were unmarried and regularly participating in Christian activities were sexually active, some with multiple partners. As a pastor, I know that the words of Paul: 'Sexual immorality . . . must not even be named among you' (5:3), are not a pronouncement from an itinerant scaremonger, but need to be heeded. Perhaps you are ensnared. Sexual sin will bring you down. It is only a matter of time before you become yet another Christian felled by one of the greatest arsenal the devil has unleashed: counterfeit love, sexual immorality.

But God, in his grace, is able to forgive and restore those who sincerely turn back to him.

3. Walk in the light (Ephesians 5:7–14)

a. As children of light (5:7–10)

Those taught in Christ should not participate in immoral lifestyles. Though once engulfed in that kind of darkness, they have now been brought into the light. As children of light, they should walk in that light, bearing the fruit of the light. Paul is urging them not only to walk in a manner that is well informed, but also in holiness. The fruit of light is pleasing to the Lord, but the fruit of darkness is too shameful even to mention.

b. Exposing the deeds of darkness (5:11–14)

The believer is therefore urged to expose the works of darkness. This is because cover-up will always lead to flare-up, while disclosure will lead to healing and restoration. Transparency is mandatory, so we need to cultivate this in the way we handle relationships with the opposite sex, in the way we handle finances, in the groups we associate with. People can present a public image while they have secret goings-on in their lives which would bring disrepute to the gospel. No-one knows about these goings-on – until there is a leak to the media. Exposure forces accountability. Let Christ shine on our lives and bring repentance and new life.

The East African revival popularized the phrase 'walking in the light'. The brethren, as they were known, used this to refer to public confessions of failures and personal decisions. If you wanted to get married, start a business or go on a journey, you were to 'walk in the light'.

Christians had an honest way of confronting anyone who was not walking in the light. Often friends would go for prayer in the bush, walking to a favourite spot. Since they would walk the same path daily, a well-beaten track would develop. If a brother or sister missed going to the place of prayer for a period of time, friends would approach them and say, 'Brother/sister, we have noticed that grass has been growing on your path.' In essence, they would be telling them to walk the familiar path again. How is your path?

4. Walk in diligence (Ephesians 5:15 – 6:9)

a. Redeeming the time

Paul invited the Ephesians to walk wisely and circumspectly. They should redeem the time: 'buying up' or 'seizing' the opportunity. The picture here is of taking advantage of something seasonal. We are living in evil days when we need to understand the will of God. When we understand the times, we will step out and grasp opportunities.

The history of missions has shown us some great missed opportunities. For example:

- When the first missionaries came to Swaziland, almost exactly a century ago, they were strongly divided along denominational lines. The king of Swaziland showed interest in the Christian faith, and wanted to learn more. He even requested the churches to come together to baptize him. But because the churches could not agree on which denomination should baptize him, they were unable to come together, and he did not learn more. The king, who held influence over the direction of the nation, remained in his traditional religion.

- We were able to provide training and resources for young church leaders in Eritrea, when the country was quite open to the proclamation of the gospel. But the gospel did not permeate to the political leaders. Now over a thousand believers, including pastors, are in jail, churches are closed, and the gospel cannot be proclaimed openly. The majority of believers have had to flee due to systematic persecution. The hope of the church in this country now lies more among its diaspora, with just a small struggling group of believers left.

Now we have a new opportunity to grasp. Are we ready to engage a Northern Sudanese country that is likely to be hostile to the proclamation of the gospel? We have three months before that window slams shut.[3] Will we look in faith, and work to buy up the time in situations like this around the world?

Opportunities are not waiting; they are passing us by. Let us redeem them now.

b. In the fullness of the Spirit

i) Impact on the Christian community:
Paul warns the believers against getting drunk with wine, but instead urges them to 'be filled with the Spirit'. As the Contemporary English Version (CEV) puts it: 'Do not destroy yourself by getting drunk.' When one is under the influence of 'liquid spirits', it can lead to self-destruction. Being filled with the Holy Spirit, by contrast, will lead to joyous celebration.

In the fellowship, there should be melody making and rejoicing in the Lord. This must have been written for Africans! No wonder we sing, 'Jabulani Africa': Sing for joy, O, Africa! We sing all the time. We sing when we are happy; we sing during funerals; we sing at political rallies; and we sing a lot at Christian gatherings.

This is more than cultural singing. It is an expression of the fullness of the Spirit. Whatever version of this you subscribe to, it should produce inspiration, encouragement and a manifestation of joy. There seems to be an exodus from the church because it is viewed as boring. The fullness of the Spirit in the fellowship might just glue people to their seats. People hunger for an encounter with the supernatural; through the vibrancy of the Holy Spirit, they can experience this. Let us seek fullness.

ii) Impact on the household:
Paul picked on familiar household ethical codes and showed them at work, not just as a cultural requirement, but because of the presence of the Lord in the lives of the believers. As believers, a higher standard was expected. With the Lord's help, they would be able to fulfil these codes of behaviour.

Husbands should therefore show sacrificial love to their wives, and not just to their congregations and strangers. This is applied in detail to the husband-wife relationship, which is a mirror or a window to let people glimpse the love of Christ for the church.

The wife likewise is urged to respect her husband. It is always tragic to see a wife reduce her husband to insignificance by belittling and despising him. And it is always a joy to see a wife make a husband scale to heights he would never have dreamed of, because she stood with him whispering, 'You can make it, you can make it!' It is also true that a lively woman can be reduced to a withered twig by a husband who is selfish, uncaring, irresponsible and unloving. And yet a husband can bring out the flower in his wife and cause her to blossom, because he cherishes, appreciates and loves her. Can your spouse testify well to your Christian walk, shown in the way you relate to each other?

This spills over to how you treat your children, your parents, your colleagues (both senior and junior). There needs to be a clear testimony to your walk with Christ in these relationships as well.

Conclusion: A porcupine and the letter of the law

The call to journey into the heart of God is a call to walk in newness of life, in love, in the light, in all diligence; to distance ourselves from anything that would mar our testimony and hinder our impact. Let us go on this journey with a true desire to please God. And let us not set our eyes only on not disobeying the letter of his law.

I finish with a story from my continent. It shows a man whose eyes do not rise above the letter of the law. Let us take it to heart as a cautionary tale.

In a certain country, the law of the land clearly stated that no man should eat a porcupine. A man was found hunting porcupines and was challenged. He replied, 'The law says you shall not *eat* a porcupine; it does not say you shall not hunt a porcupine.' Found carrying a porcupine, he was asked the same question. 'The law says you shall not *eat* a porcupine; it does not say you shall not carry one.' Found skinning a porcupine, he responded, 'The law says you shall not *eat* a porcupine, it does not say you shall not skin it.' Found roasting a porcupine, he responded, 'The law says you shall not *eat* a porcupine; it does not say you shall not roast it.' Found tasting a porcupine, he responded, 'The law says you shall not *eat* a porcupine; it does not say you shall not taste it.'

Unfortunately, in the end, he tasted the *whole* porcupine!

Some of us may be struggling in our walk with the Lord. A problem started out as something small, but has now got out of control. You may have gone too far. Do not justify it by looking to the letter of the law. You know in your heart what is right. Walk in the light. Turn back to the Lord and ask his forgiveness. May our walk be a journey that will truly lead us into the heart of God.

Calisto Odede is senior pastor of Nairobi Pentecostal Church, Woodley, Kenya. www.citam.org

CALLING THE CHURCH BACK TO HUMILITY, INTEGRITY, SIMPLICITY
Chris Wright (UK)

We have been thinking firstly of the *gospel* itself, as God's truth in the person of Jesus, and as God's reconciling power; and secondly of the *world*, with all its confusion of religions and needs. But what about ourselves, the church of Christ? What kind of people must we be?

About 4,000 years ago, God gave the Great Commission to Abraham, telling him to 'go . . . be a blessing . . . and through you all nations on the earth will be blessed'. That is God's great mission. That, says Paul, is the gospel the Scriptures announced in advance to Abraham: God will bless the nations!

God's plan was that this should happen by God first creating a people, his own people, a people chosen in Abraham, redeemed through Christ, and called to 'keep the way of the LORD by doing righteousness and justice', so that God could keep his promise to Abraham and bless all nations through him (Genesis 18:19). That's why I chose Abraham, God says. The whole purpose of our election is missional and ethical, as we were reminded from Ephesians 1. We are to live out the fruit of our predestination by living to the praise of God's glory.

God has kept his promise to bless the nations. Many Gentiles in the Old Testament came to faith in the living God and came into his blessing – Rahab, Ruth, Naaman, for example. There were many more in the New Testament, and we can trace the story on through the history of the church. God has been keeping his promise to Abraham right up to today. That is God's great mission.

There were many obstacles – in Bible times and since – to frustrate and hinder that great loving, saving mission of God: challenges we need to overcome as we participate with God in his mission.

What do you think is the greatest of those obstacles to God's desire for the evangelization of the world?

I do not believe it is other religions, or persecution, or resistant cultures, serious challenges though those all are. But the overwhelming witness of the Bible is that the greatest problem for God in his redemptive mission for the world is his own people. What hurts God most, it seems, is not just the sin of the world, but the failure, disobedience and rebellion of those God has redeemed and called to be his people, his holy distinctive people.

Have you noticed that the vast bulk of words in the books of the prophets were addressed to God's own people, Israel, and only a few chapters to 'oracles against the nations'? By contrast, we tend to spend our time attacking and complaining about the world, and ignoring our own failures.

The greatest problem for God is his own people.

Think for a moment about Old Testament Israel:

- God called them to be 'a light to the nations'. But according to Ezekiel (5:6; 16:44–52), Israel sank even lower than the nations, including Sodom and Gomorrah: 'She has rebelled against my laws and decrees more than the nations and countries around her.'
- God called them into the great blessing of redemption and covenant, into the great privilege of being called to know him as the one true living God, to love and worship him alone. But constantly they went after other gods, falling into repeated idolatry.

Idolatry is the biggest single obstacle to world mission. For if God's mission is to bring all nations into the blessing of knowing and worshipping him alone as Creator and Redeemer, then the greatest threat to that is the worship of other gods, false gods, no gods. The problem was not just the idolatry of the foreign nations, but the idolatry of God's own people.

Many false gods and idols entice us away from the living God alone, but three seem especially seductive for evangelical Christians today, as they were for Israel of old: (i) the idol of power and pride; (ii) the idol of popularity and success; (iii) the idol of wealth and greed. The Old Testament prophets, Jesus and the apostles all give us powerful warnings against these three terrible idols that pollute and pervert the mission of God's people.

1. The idol of power and pride

Listen to the Word of the Lord, through Isaiah:

> The LORD Almighty has a day in store
>   for all the proud and lofty,
>   for all that is exalted
>   (and they will be humbled) . . .
> The arrogance of man will be brought low
>   and the pride of men humbled;
> the LORD alone will be exalted in that day,
>   and the idols will totally disappear.
> (Isaiah 2:12, 17–18)

Listen to the great requirement through Micah:

> And what does the LORD require of you?
> To act justly and to love mercy
>   and to walk humbly with your God.
> (Micah 6:8)

Listen to the Lord Jesus Christ himself:

> Jesus said to them, 'The kings of the Gentiles lord it over them . . . But you are not to be like that. Instead, the greatest among you should be like the youngest, and the one who rules like the one who serves . . . I am among you as one who serves.'
> (Luke 22:25–27)

And as we saw in our Bible exposition on Ephesians 4, when Paul
talks about the life that is worthy of our calling in the gospel, he
urges, 'Be completely humble and gentle; be patient, bearing with
one another in love' (Ephesians 4:2).

To be obsessed with power and status in Christian work is sheer
disobedience to Christ and the Bible. It destroys the very thing we
are trying to accomplish. We are called back in repentance to *Humility*.

2. The idols of popularity and success

These idols lead us into manipulation, dishonesty, distortion –
like the false prophets who were claiming to speak the Word of
God, but were really acting in self-interest, claiming to be men
of God, but were just giving the people whatever they most wanted
to hear or see at the time. They were popular and successful
certainly, but they were false prophets in the grip of a false god.

Listen to the Word of God through Jeremiah:

> From the least to the greatest,
>   all are greedy for gain;
> prophets and priests alike,
>   all practise deceit.
> They dress the wound of my people
>   as though it were not serious.
> 'Peace, peace,' they say,
>   when there is no peace.
> Are they ashamed of their loathsome conduct?
>   No, they have no shame at all;
>   they do not even know how to blush.
> (Jeremiah 6:13–15)

Have some of us lost that sense of shame, and even the ability to
blush?

Even in the early church, Paul warned against those who 'peddled
the word of God for profit', those who 'used deception and distortion' (2 Corinthians 2:17; 4:2). The church was dazzled by these

'super-apostles' as he called them, who boasted of their credentials, their impressive speaking, their great popularity. They were the kind of successful leaders the church at Corinth wanted – to boost their own image. But Paul says,

> Such men are false apostles, deceitful workmen, masquerading as apostles of Christ. And no wonder, for Satan himself masquerades as an angel of light. It is not surprising, then, if his servants masquerade as servants of righteousness. Their end will be what their actions deserve.
> (2 Corinthians 11:13–15)

We cannot build the kingdom of the God of truth on foundations of dishonesty. Telling lies about our success, or accepting what we know to be very questionable statistics, in order to obtain or to grant funding for projects, is nothing short of bowing down to the idols of manipulated success. We are called back in repentance to *Integrity*.

3. The idols of wealth and greed

The idolatry of greed infected the religious leaders of Israel too.
Listen to the Lord's Word through Micah:

> Her leaders judge for a bribe,
>   her priests teach for a price,
>   and her prophets tell fortunes for money.
> (Micah 3:11)

Isaiah saw in his day, as in ours, a whole culture of greed, accumulation and covetousness. Paul says twice that greed *is* idolatry.

> Woe to you who add house to house
>   and join field to field
> till no space is left
>   and you live alone in the land.
> (Isaiah 5:8)

Of course, we know that God provides abundantly for his people. But Moses, who rejoiced in that expectation, also warned against the danger:

> When you eat and are satisfied, when you build fine houses and settle down, and when your herds and flocks grow large and your silver and gold increase and all you have is multiplied, then your heart will become proud and you will forget the LORD your God, who brought you out of Egypt, out of the land of slavery. (Deuteronomy 8:12–14)

Jesus gave the same stern warning: 'Watch out! Be on your guard against all kinds of greed; a man's life does not consist in the abundance of his possessions' (Luke 12:15). Neither, he could have added, does a man's ministry. We are called back in repentance to *Simplicity*.

Jesus himself faced the same three temptations:

- The devil offered him power and status over all nations, from a high mountain. Jesus refused these, choosing to worship God alone. Jesus chose the path of humility.
- The devil suggested he manipulate the crowds by a spectacular death-defying miracle. Jesus recognized the way Satan was twisting Scripture to get him to achieve success. Jesus chose the path of integrity in his trust in God.
- The devil dangled before him the lucrative prospect of abundant food for himself and the hungry masses – turn stones into bread, you could make a fortune for yourself with such a miracle! Jesus resisted with the scriptural truth that God could supply bread, but human beings need greater food for life than that. Jesus chose the path of simplicity in dependence on the promises of God.

So Jesus resisted these temptations to give in to the false gods.

But tragically, it seems that so many Christian leaders (including mission leaders) blatantly *fail* these tests at precisely the points that

Jesus overcame them. They cannot resist the temptations of elevated
status, manipulated success and selfish greed. And then the whole
church pays the cost of their failure, in the loss of integrity and credibility. So whenever we point a finger of criticism at the sin of the
world, we are told, bluntly and rightly, 'Clean up your own back yard.'
We are, in short, a scandal, a stumbling block, to the mission of God.

Look back to the Reformation in Europe. Why was it needed?
In the medieval church in Europe, we see these three idols masquer-
ading in the corrupt ecclesiastical system:

- Powerful prince bishops, wielding enormous wealth and power
- Shrines and saints that were very popular and successful for
  church income
- People making their fortune from selling indulgences –
  exploiting the poor with promises of good things in the life
  to come

Meanwhile, ordinary people lived in ignorance of the Bible, which
wasn't available in their language and wasn't being preached from
the pulpits. Reformation was the desperate need of the hour.

Surely we face the same desperate need now. And, I dare to
propose, it must begin in the worldwide evangelical community. For
there are parts of the so-called evangelical church today where the
same three idols are rampant:

- There are self-appointed 'super-apostles' and other mighty
  and elevated leaders, unaccountable to anybody, popular with
  thousands of followers, lording it over the flock of Christ,
  unconcerned for the weak and poor, showing none of the
  marks of an apostle that Paul talks about, and with no
  resemblance to the crucified Christ. That's the idolatry of
  pride and power.
- There is a craze for 'success', for 'results', the largest
  number in the shortest time. There is an obsession with
  statistics and outcomes, which sometimes leads to wild claims,

unsubstantiated numbers, untrue reports – blatant
manipulation and collusion in falsehood, all for the sake of
funding and so forth. That's the idolatry of success.

- There is the so-called 'prosperity gospel'. We certainly affirm
what the Bible says about God's blessing, about the power of
God's Spirit and the victory of God over all that crushes
and curses human life, but, as Femi Adeleye will attest (see
p. 159ff.), many promoters of this teaching distort the Bible
(if they use it at all), appeal to human greed, have no place
for the Bible's teaching on suffering and taking up the cross,
and succeed only in enriching themselves, in a lifestyle utterly
contrary to the teaching and example of Christ. This is the
idolatry of greed.

Meanwhile, as in pre-Reformation Europe, the ordinary people of
God in so many churches live in ignorance of the Bible, with pastors
who neither know it themselves nor are willing or able to preach
and teach it. Reformation is once again the desperate need. And it
needs to start with us.

So what must we do? We need a radical return to the Lord. We
need to hear the prophetic word, from the prophets and apostles
of God, and from the Lord Jesus Christ himself: 'Repent, and believe
the gospel . . . ' Remember, Jesus preached *that* message, made that
command – *not* to pagan unbelievers, Gentile outsiders, people of
other faiths – but to those who already claimed to be God's covenant
people. And so it comes to us.

- Before we go out to the world, we must come back to the
Lord.
- If we want to change the world, we must first change our
own hearts and ways (Jeremiah 7:3–8).
- As we take the words of the gospel to the world, we must
also take with us words of confession to God (Hosea 14:1–2).
- When we get off our seats to seek the lost, we must first get
on our knees to seek the Lord.

I invite you to do these things – in prayer before God. Where we have been exalted because of our status, titles or authority, let us walk humbly with our God, for the Lord gives grace to the humble, but puts down the proud. Where we have manipulated, distorted or exaggerated, let us walk in the light and truth of God, for the Lord looks on the heart and is pleased with integrity. Where we have used our ministry for our own selfish gain, let us walk in the simplicity of Jesus, for we cannot serve God and mammon.

Let us declare ourselves HIS people through the way we live.

Let us declare ourselves HIS people through the way we live: as people of Humility, Integrity and Simplicity. Let us be what we are, for God's sake, for our mission's sake, for the world's sake.

Conclusion

Our mission demands that the church itself must be an authentic model of what we preach, demonstrating what it means to live as a community of reconciled love and unity.

This is what Jesus repeated emphatically four times in John's Gospel in his last conversation with his disciples before his death. It's what we've been hearing from Paul in Ephesians. All three terrible idolatries will destroy that unity. The primary cause of our disunity and fragmentation is our obsession with these things. People who build and defend their own status and power will not unite in humility with others. People who have no integrity in what they do and say cannot be trusted in the costly work of transparency and unity. People who are motivated by selfishness see other Christian ministries as competition. Humility, integrity, simplicity are the signposts to unity; and unity is a pre-condition of our mission, according to Jesus, in his command and his prayer.

Again we come to the double challenge of (i) the need for radical obedient discipleship, leading to maturity: growth in depth as well as growth in numbers; and (ii) the need for radical cross-centred reconciliation, leading to unity: growth in love as well as growth in faith and hope. Both are commanded by Jesus and his apostles and indispensable to our mission. There is no biblical mission without biblical living.

Chris Wright was Chair of the Cape Town 2010 statement committee which worked to produce The Cape Town Commitment. *He is International Director of The Langham Partnership, and a senior advisor to the Lausanne Theology Working Group, of which he is a former Chair.*

THE PROSPERITY GOSPEL
Femi Adeleye (Nigeria)

The best starting point for a lifestyle of humility, integrity and simplicity is to remain faithful to the gospel and contend for the faith as it was 'once for all delivered to the saints' (Jude 3). For what the church believes and practises depends on how Scripture is read and interpreted. Remaining true to the gospel was so important to the apostle Paul, that he warned the church in the provinces of Galatia:

> I am astonished that you are so quickly deserting the one who called you by the grace of Christ and are turning to a different gospel – which is really no gospel at all. Evidently some people are throwing you into confusion and are trying to pervert the gospel of Christ. But even if we or an angel from heaven should preach a gospel other than the one we preached to you, let him be eternally condemned!
> (Galatians 1:6–8)

This warning remains true for us today. For we live in times when the church has been infiltrated by 'different gospels', one of the fastest-growing and prominent of which is the 'prosperity gospel', sometimes known as the 'health-and-wealth gospel'.

What is the 'prosperity gospel'?

This 'gospel' asserts that believers have the right to the blessings of health and wealth, and can obtain them through confessions of faith and the 'sowing of seeds' (payments of tithes and offerings). The Bible affirms that God cares enough for his people to bless and provide for their needs, and that there are legitimate ways to work for those needs to be met. But this gospel makes the pursuit of material things and physical well-being an end in itself.

The 'health-and-wealth gospel' has spread to most parts of our world and across denominations. It focuses primarily on material possessions, physical well-being and success in this life. This includes abundant financial resources, good health, good clothes, good housing, cars, promotion at work, success in examinations and business. The extent of material acquisition and well-being is often interpreted as a sign of one's good standing before God. Scripture is interpreted or manipulated to promote this.

For example, Luke 6:38 is commonly used to motivate congregations to give: 'Give, and it will be given to you: good measure, pressed down, shaken together, and running over, will be put into your bosom. For with the same measure that you use, it will be measured back to you.' This verse is found in the context of Jesus' teaching on love and mercy, and how we should relate to others. The paragraph begins in verse 37: 'Judge not, and you shall not be judged. Condemn not, and you shall not be condemned. Forgive, and you will be forgiven.' Following God's example of love and mercy, believers should be hesitant in judging others, and realize that God will treat them in the way they have treated others. So the passage is about relationships and how we treat others. For in this regard, 'with the same measure [we] use, it will be measured back to [us]'.

The text is not about giving to God financially, nor expecting returns for what we give. Yet it is twisted to indicate that God will multiply whatever one gives in offerings. Few who use this passage to motivate people to give would refer to the unusually strong words of the Lord Jesus Christ earlier in the same chapter. Yet in Luke 6:24–25 Jesus says,

> But woe to you who are rich,
>   for you have received your consolation.
> Woe to you who are full,
>   for you shall hunger.
> Woe to you who laugh now,
>   for you shall mourn and weep.

Some use 3 John 2: 'I pray that you may prosper in all things' as a mandate for the prosperity gospel. The word used for 'prosper' in

English comes from the Greek *euodoō*, which means 'good road, route or journey'. So the apostle says, 'I want you to have a good and healthy lifelong journey.' The words do not refer to riches or wealth. Why would John, a witness of the life of Christ say, 'Above everything else, I want you to be rich or wealthy'?

The reference to abundant life in John 10:10 is also used. The term for life here is *zōē*, a word indicating 'life in the spirit and soul', rather than *bios*, which is used to refer to physical, material life. Jesus is saying, 'I want you to have an abundant life in the Spirit.' He is not referring to riches, cars, houses and designer clothes.

This 'different gospel':

- *distorts the mission of Jesus as primarily to save from sin.* Some prosperity preachers teach that Jesus has come, both to save people from their sin *and* to make them rich, but it is rare to hear preaching on repentance or salvation from sin in health-and-wealth gospel circles.
- *fails to see that all forms of giving to God are primarily acts of worship.* Instead, it teaches that tithing or giving to God is an investment that must yield returns. It pressurizes people to give with wrong motives: for returns or rewards here and now in material form.
- *distorts the person of Christ.* Some preachers portray Jesus as being materially rich. While Jesus was not a destitute, we know from Scripture that he was not rich.
- *feeds on greed.* It feeds on the greed of its teachers at the expense of the needs of their followers.
- *lacks an explanation for the suffering of believers.* Either it is silent about this or it explains it as being through lack of faith, or sin.

We often see more energy spent in raising money than in working to present the true gospel, or nourishing the spiritual health of God's people. This is a travesty of the role of the pastor and teacher, and demonstrates that, to them, money is more important than people or the urgent task of evangelism.

Jesus did not preach or teach a prosperity gospel. All that he taught about earthly possession comes as a warning to us. He taught very clearly: 'Take heed and beware of covetousness, for one's life does not consist in the abundance of the things he possesses' (Luke 12:15). Jesus also warned against the deceitfulness of riches (Matthew 13:22), and refers to an 'unrighteous mammon' (Luke 16:9). As an end in itself, money will compete for our loyalty to God and become an idol that rules our lives: 'No servant can serve two masters; for either he will hate the one and love the other, or else he will be loyal to the one and despise the other. You cannot serve God and mammon' (Luke 16:13).

The hermeneutics of this gospel raises other questions. Does it affirm and point people to the cross? Is the lifestyle of its proponents consistent with a cross-centred faith?

There are many casualties of this 'gospel' who have become disillusioned with the real gospel because they have sown their seed-faith and not seen promised fruits.

Is the prosperity gospel good news for the poor?
The prosperity gospel presents itself as offering advocacy for the poor, but is hardly good news for them. Often the shepherds are fleecing the flock. The poor who sow the seed do not get richer, while the leaders and pastors wear better suits, drive better cars and acquire bigger homes.

There is a deep sense of injustice and immorality here, when one considers the severe plight of the poor who are often very vulnerable. Some who keep 'sowing to the prosperity gospel' can hardly afford regular meals themselves, or other basic essentials such as shelter or school fees for their children. Most of us live in contexts where even new-born babies are being abandoned on the streets by mothers who have no means of supporting them. It is iniquitous that such people should be manipulated to support affluent lifestyles.

Followers of Jesus cannot support a gospel that aligns itself with Hollywood's celebrity culture, and deprives the poor of dignity and respect, where preachers connive and dangle unrealistic shortcuts to prosperity, rather than helping others to improve their situations through work, resilience and endurance. Poverty alleviation and advocacy for the poor have become a multi-billion-dollar business, but the poor in many contexts are not benefiting. This is an affront to the poor, and to God. Not only is the prosperity gospel a false delusion, but ultimately it distracts from the true gospel of God's saving grace through Jesus Christ, reducing God to the 'genie in the bottle' who can be manipulated at will.

To embrace this gospel is to fall into the peril of the love of money (2 Timothy 3:1–5). The kingdom of God is not 'of this world'.

How should we respond?

In his book, *Money & Power*, the French theologian Jacques Ellul argues that 'money is power, a spirit, a would-be god, a rival master'. He distinguishes between money and wealth:

> Wealth consists of the good things of God's creation, meant for our enjoyment. Money is the world's way of amassing those things, hoarding them, assuring that you can have more tomorrow, and dividing people according to its arbitrary rules. Money does not merely tempt, it engulfs. It spins its web around people, forcing them into its service. [4]

Few can speak as authoritatively on the prosperity gospel as the televangelist Jim Bakker. In an interview with *Charisma*, shortly after his release from jail, he admitted building a 1980s-style tower of Babel to make a name for himself. This tower was a multimillion-dollar business with a $30 million payroll and 2,200 staff. Bakker has since repented. His book, *I Was Wrong*, teaches about sacrifice and the cost of discipleship. But in the interview he says,

> While I was in prison, the Lord showed me he wanted me to study the words of Christ in the Bible. So I began to write out in longhand every word that Christ had spoken. I spent two years

doing this. I wanted to know Christ and everything he had said. And as I began to absorb the teachings of Christ, it changed my life. Sometimes I would be moved to study sixteen hours a day.

What did Bakker discover about wealth?

While I studied Jesus' words, I couldn't find anywhere in the Bible where he had said anything good about money. And this started to prick my heart. Luke 6:24 says, 'Woe to you who are rich.' Jesus talked about the 'deceitfulness of riches' in Mark 4:19. Jesus told us not to lay up treasures on earth in Matthew 6:24. In Luke 12:15, he said, 'Watch out! Be on your guard against all kinds of greed; a man's life does not consist in the abundance of his possessions.'

We need to take the plight of the poor seriously enough to reject this false gospel. We should all feel a sense of pain as we see a part of the church drifting away from sound doctrine. Some have turned the sacred space of the pulpit into a shrine of mammon-worship. It was injustice and idolatry of greed that made our Lord use such strong words against the rich, and it was this which moved him to express his anger physically, in the only such instance recorded for us, in the temple.

Let us take seriously the truth from Uncle John Stott that: 'Life, in fact, is a pilgrimage from one moment of nakedness to another. So we should travel lightly and live simply.'

Have we used the gospel, or Christian ministry, to idolize material things, or to acquire more things than we need? Have we eaten more food than we need? Or twisted Scripture to justify our lifestyles? Let us repent and return to the simplicity and compassion of Christ.

Femi Adeleye is IFES Associate General Secretary for Partnership and Collaboration. www.ifesworld.org

HUMAN SEXUALITY, BY GOD'S DESIGN

Walk in love, rejecting the idolatry of disordered sexuality
(Ephesians 5:1–7).

God's design in creation is that marriage is constituted by
the committed, faithful relationship between one man and
one woman, in which they become one flesh in a new social
unity that is distinct from their birth families, and that sexual
intercourse as the expression of that 'one flesh' is to be
enjoyed exclusively within the bond of marriage. This loving
sexual union within marriage, in which 'two become one',
reflects both Christ's relationship with the church and also
the unity of Jew and Gentile in the new humanity.[5]

Paul contrasts the purity of God's love with the ugliness of
counterfeit love that masquerades in disordered sexuality and
all that goes along with it. Disordered sexuality of all kinds, in
any practice of sexual intimacy before or outside marriage as
biblically defined, is out of line with God's will and blessing in
creation and redemption. The abuse and idolatry that surround
disordered sexuality contribute to wider social decline,
including the breakdown of marriages and families, and
produce incalculable suffering of loneliness and exploitation.
It is a serious issue within the church itself, and it is a tragically
common cause of leadership failure.

We recognize our need for deep humility and consciousness
of failure in this area. We long to see Christians challenging our
surrounding cultures by living according to the standards to
which the Bible calls us.

a) We strongly encourage all pastors:

    i. To facilitate more open conversation about sexuality
      in our churches, declaring positively the good news
      of God's plan for healthy relationships and family

life, but also addressing with pastoral honesty the areas where Christians share in the broken and dysfunctional realities of their surrounding culture;

ii. To teach God's standards clearly, but to do so with Christ's pastoral compassion for sinners, recognizing how vulnerable we all are to sexual temptation and sin;

iii. To strive to set a positive example in living by biblical standards of sexual faithfulness.

b) As members of the church, we commit ourselves:

i. To do all we can in the church and in society to strengthen faithful marriages and healthy family life;

ii. To recognize the presence and contribution of those who are single, widowed or childless, to ensure the church is a welcoming and sustaining family in Christ, and to enable them to exercise their gifts in the full range of the church's ministries;

iii. To resist the multiple forms of disordered sexuality in our surrounding cultures, including pornography, adultery and promiscuity;

iv. To seek to understand and address the deep heart issues of identity and experience which draw some people into homosexual practice; to reach out with the love, compassion and justice of Christ, and to reject and condemn all forms of hatred, verbal or physical abuse, and victimization of homosexual people;

v. To remember that by God's redemptive grace, no person or situation is beyond the possibility of change and restoration.

Cape Town Commitment IIE2

DAY 6

PARTNERSHIP: Partnering in the body of Christ towards a new global equilibrium

TESTIMONY: TRANSFORMATION IN THE GARBAGE VILLAGE
Rebecca Atallah (Egypt)

Anyone looking at the Moqattam garbage village in Cairo today would have a hard time believing what it was like when I first went there in 1982. At that time, people lived with their animals and their garbage, bathing their children, cooking their food, all sleeping together. They had no electricity or running water, no churches, no schools. In fact, they had no services of any kind except for drugs and alcohol, and there was a lot of both.

The people were nominally Christian, but had no idea of God's love for them. In fact, they basically considered themselves garbage. Evil and violence reigned. But now it is all very different. As you go in, you see high-rise buildings, schools, churches, services of every kind, markets. These tell a story.

So what brought about this change, in one generation? The answer is that the Holy Spirit used one simple layman, who took them one simple message: God loves you. This man first led his garbage man to the Lord. Then, on repeated insistence from this garbage man, he went to the village and started sharing Jesus with this man's family and friends. He found that the people were very responsive to this wonderful message of God's love for them.

This man, used by God as an evangelist to these people, had no money, no social programmes. But through the power of the Holy Spirit, defeating the evil spirits, many professed faith in Christ, and miracles followed. The garbage collector, still young in the faith, had some great prayer warriors behind him, including one American man who knew very little Arabic, but who prayed faithfully every day for him and his family.

As the number of believers grew, the Coptic Orthodox leaders built them a small church. Not surprisingly, its members wanted this layman, who had brought them the gospel, to be their pastor. He was ordained and became Abuna Samaan, Father Simon.

As the church grew, people were changed completely from the inside out by the Holy Spirit. He gave them a different motivation, and new desires to use their money to build homes instead of buying alcohol. They asked for a school and help in building classrooms, so that their kids could learn to read the Bible, even though they couldn't read themselves. They became great recyclers, and today are some of the best in the world. They were still garbage collectors, living in what was at that stage the same smelly village, but they were now motivated by the love and power of Jesus Christ.

Then the Holy Spirit led them in rather miraculous ways to discover caves in their village, just a little further up in the mountain. These are now the world-famous cave churches of Egypt. The biggest one seats up to 20,000 people. That makes it the largest church in the Middle East.

Thousands from inside and outside the village go every week to services in these cave churches. One of Father Simon's favourite verses has become a reality in the garbage village: 'God chose the weak things of the world to shame the strong. He chose the lowly things of this world and the despised things . . . to nullify the things that are' (1 Corinthians 1:28). It is because of God's work in Father Simon, an ordinary, weak man, that the garbage village people are believing in Christ Jesus.

Now we are building a large, fully equipped centre for the disabled and the chronically ill, another very marginalized group in Egyptian society. And Salawah, one of the founding members of this ministry, is the daughter of Father Simon's garbage man.

Rebecca Atallah is active in helping with the Christian education programme in Moqattam village, and with ministry among Sudanese refugees.

EPHESIANS 6:10–24
Ramez Atallah (Egypt)

Equipping the church for service

In the mid-1970s, Lindsay Brown, Lausanne International Director, was serving with Operation Mobilization (OM). The ministry of the ship *Doulos* had been very successful, and they were praying at an all-night prayer meeting that the Lord would provide them with another ship.

At 1 am they received a telegram from the leadership of Youth With A Mission (YWAM), an organization similar to OM. Hearing about OM's need, they had prayed. They had collected money to purchase a ship themselves, but the deals they had tried to negotiate had fallen through. So they decided to give all the money they had collected to OM.

In the 1970s, that story inspired us to believe that shrewd, entrepreneurial evangelicals can rejoice in other people's ministry, encourage others and even give their hard-earned money to other organizations.

In the past few days, we have feasted on Ephesians. In chapter 1 we were amazed by the blessing of being included in God's great plan of salvation through the gospel. In Ephesians 2, we understood that, when God reconciles alienated people to himself and to one another, he incorporates them into this beautiful body which we call the church. In Ephesians 3, we learned how God's wisdom and glory are made known to the demonic power of the universe, for the church as it suffers and prays. In Ephesians 4:1–16, we learned that the church needs to be faithful to the ministry of the Word, marked by the unity and maturity that God desires. In Ephesians 5, we saw how the church is called to be distinct from the world, in lifestyle and relationships.

Now we're going to look at spiritual warfare. No-one today questions that Christians are engaged in this, or indeed that we are recipients of attack. But too often we use the world's weapons instead of God's. In Ephesians 6, we learn how to use God's weapons, his equipment rather than the world's. This passage helps us to identify our true enemies, and to protect ourselves against them.

The passage is divided into two sections: our responsibility (verses 10–13) and God's equipment or God's weapons (verses 14–20). These weapons are divinely empowered by the same power that raised Jesus from the dead, but we must take the initiative in using them.

In the light of our high calling, Paul is concerned that we maintain this glorious faith. He concludes his letter with counsel on how to do so. The armour of God is the only equipment which can help us take our stand again the devil's attacks. Paul yearns for people who will not abandon the faith. 'I don't want you to be weaklings; I want you to be strong: therefore put on the whole armour of God. Put on this armour, so that you may be able to stand against the schemes of the devil. Put it on and stand firm.'

Many Christians don't withstand the devil's schemes. They either lose the wonder of the gospel and grow cold, or they simply fall away. [Ramez Atallah asked at this point for a brief interlude for prayer: for family, friends and Christian leaders who have not stood firm. He concluded: 'Father, you've heard our yearning, the yearning of our hearts, for these brothers and sisters all over the world who have not stood. We pray that you may restore them and that you would help us to stand. Amen.']

Paul reminds us that our struggle is against the devil and his schemes, but not against flesh and blood, for we do not wrestle against these (verse 12). Yet we are often threatened by those who have a different point of view. We have narrow eyes, and we need to remember that the invisible church of Jesus Christ is very much bigger than we can imagine, and includes many more than those whom we might define as evangelicals.

'[We wrestle] against the rulers . . . against the cosmic powers over this present darkness, against the spiritual forces of evil in the heavenly places.' These forces have attacked this Congress while we've been here, but because of spiritual warfare in prayer by many, the Lord has graciously stopped them and helped us to continue.[1] We thank God for that.

As we consider how to put on the full armour of God, we'll look at three 'essentials': essential values, essential beliefs and essential resources.

Essential values. Here we have: (i) the belt of truth. If we're not convinced by the truth of our gospel, we cannot engage in spiritual warfare or defend the gospel; (ii) the breastplate of righteousness, to protect our hearts for integrity; and (iii) the shoes of the gospel of peace, to reflect the peace between us and God, and to make peace between us and our fellow men. How the world needs peacemakers!

I've watched this Congress behind the scenes. One of the reasons why it has gone so smoothly is because the hundreds of volunteers involved in running it have exhibited these essential values, even under immense pressure. We have had CEOs and high school graduates, all working together in humility and love: a remarkable testimony of walking the talk.

Essential beliefs. We must take up the shield of faith: exercising faith is our part. We need faith that will (i) trust in God as a loving, heavenly Father; (ii) give us a vision for the great things to which he is calling us, that he can accomplish through us; and (iii) be courageous enough to take risk, for his sake.

When we come to the helmet of salvation, 'receive' is a better translation than 'take'. It's God who gives it. He restores us to himself through the amazing plan of salvation that we've seen so wondrously in Ephesians as a whole.

Essential resources. Essential values provide us with integrity; essential beliefs give us the inner workings of our faith; essential resources keep us on our way. The Word of God and prayer are both essential resources. We provide the Bible to people of all Christian traditions in Egypt. It unites people, and therefore gives us a common presence in a Muslim country. By advertising the Bible as a product on sale to 10 million Christians in Egypt, we are placing the Scriptures in the public arena, attracting others to the gospel of Jesus Christ.

We must take up the sword of the Spirit, the Word, and we must pray in the Spirit. Paul urges us to pray on all occasions, for all people. He asks for prayers for himself twice (verses 19, 20), as he longs that he may be bold in declaring the gospel to his captors. Even the apostle Paul needed the prayers of Christians when he was in prison and tempted and in such difficulty. He didn't ask for prayer for comfort, or that he should not be mistreated. His passion until the end of his lifetime was singular: to fulfil God's calling to declare the gospel of Jesus Christ. Is this your passion? May we stand firm together in this calling, for God's glory.

Ramez Atallah, General Secretary of the Bible Society of Egypt, served as Programme Chairman for The Third Lausanne Congress. www.bsoe.org

UNREACHED AND UNENGAGED PEOPLES

The heart of God longs that *all* people should have access to the knowledge of God's love and of his saving work through Jesus Christ. We recognize with grief and shame that there are thousands of people groups around the world for whom such access has not yet been made available through Christian witness. These are peoples who are *unreached*, in the sense that there are no known believers and no churches among them. Many of these peoples are also *unengaged*, in the sense that we currently know of no churches or agencies that are even trying to share the gospel with them. Indeed, only a tiny percentage of the church's resources (human and material) is being directed to the least-reached peoples. By definition, these are peoples who will not invite us to come with the good news, since they know nothing about it. Yet their presence among us in our world, 2,000 years after Jesus commanded us to make disciples of all nations, constitutes not only a rebuke to our disobedience, not only a form of spiritual injustice, but also a silent 'Macedonian call'.

Let us rise up as the church worldwide to meet this challenge, and:

A. Repent of our blindness to the continuing presence of so many unreached peoples in our world and our lack of urgency in sharing the gospel among them.

B. Renew our commitment to go to those who have not yet heard the gospel, to engage deeply with their language and culture, to live the gospel among them with incarnational love and sacrificial service, to communicate the light and truth of the Lord Jesus Christ in word and deed, awakening them through the Holy Spirit's power to the surprising grace of God.

C. Aim to eradicate Bible poverty in the world, for the Bible remains indispensable for evangelism. To do this we must:

  1. Hasten the translation of the Bible into the languages of peoples who do not yet have any portion of God's Word in their mother tongue;

  2. Make the message of the Bible widely available by oral means.

D. Aim to eradicate Bible ignorance in the church, for the Bible remains indispensable for discipling believers into the likeness of Christ.

  1. We long to see a fresh conviction, gripping all God's church, of the central necessity of Bible teaching for the church's growth in ministry, unity and maturity (Ephesians 4:11–12). We rejoice in the gifting of all those whom Christ has given to the church as pastor-teachers. We will make every effort to identify, encourage, train and support them in the preaching and teaching of God's Word. In doing so, however, we must reject the kind of clericalism that restricts the ministry of God's Word to a few paid professionals, or to formal preaching in church pulpits. Many men and women, who are clearly gifted in pastoring and teaching God's people, exercise their gifting informally or without official denominational structures, but with the manifest blessing of God's Spirit. They too need to be recognized, encouraged and equipped rightly to handle the Word of God.

  2. We must promote Bible literacy among the generation that now relates primarily to digital communication rather than books, by encouraging digital methods of studying the Scriptures inductively

with the depth of inquiry that at present requires paper, pens and pencils.

E. Let us keep evangelism at the centre of the fully integrated scope of all our mission, inasmuch as the gospel itself is the source, content and authority of all biblically valid mission. All we do should be both an embodiment and a declaration of the love and grace of God and his saving work through Jesus Christ.

The Cape Town Commitment IID1[2]

WORKING TOWARDS A NEW
GLOBAL EQUILIBRIUM
Patrick Fung (Singapore)

Partnership is not primarily about us. It's about God and his mission. The whole church belongs to God, and this world, so dear to God's heart, also belongs to him. The mission of God's people is to declare the whole gospel to the whole world. The book of Ephesians has enriched our grasp of this. Together, as a body of Christ, we have received every spiritual blessing in Jesus Christ in the heavenly realms. And we have been given this glorious task of making known to the world the manifold wisdom of God, the many-coloured dimensions of God to the world. What we do together not only has an impact on the world, but on the rulers and authorities in the heavenly realms, a cosmic dimension.

'Equilibrium', equalizing or balancing different influences, while necessary, is not the goal of partnership. The goal is rather about God's concern for his broken world, to bring all men and women to himself, for his glory. I'm going to look at three different perspectives: God's power, God's redemption and God's sovereignty.

God's power. The biblical concept of mission is not primarily about the equilibrium of power, but about the power of God given to his people through his Spirit in the bold proclamation of the gospel of Jesus Christ. If anything, it is about the *im*balance of power, the power of God given to his people, who in people's eyes are powerless: for we are the *recipients* of that power. As we look at the early church, the advance of the gospel was not dependent on charismatic leaders, or any grand strategies, or any powerful resources. The evangelists were the nameless, 'powerless' people, who acknowledged the lordship of Christ and told others of him, often at great cost.

I can understand why The Lausanne Movement is concerned about global equilibrium. We come from different parts of the world. Some of us have great power in the world's eyes, whether financial, organizational or political. But, as Samuel Escobar passionately argued, imperialism should have no place in the missionary and theological tasks we have been given. So in the concept and practice of mission, the idea that the powerful bring the good news to the powerless must be challenged.

But our goal is not global equilibrium. The Lausanne Movement was founded as the LCWE: the Lausanne Committee for World Evangelization, not the Lausanne Committee for World Equilibrium. Making disciples of all nations must be our most urgent and ultimate goal.

I want to take us back to examples from the early church. Generosity was always a way of life there. It was always sharing, and there was always interdependence. The church in Antioch supported the church in Jerusalem. There was both a willingness to give and a humility to receive. The sharing of God's resources must be mutual and not one-directional. Let me say this very carefully: A one-directional, over-enthusiastic giving, which leads to over-receiving with greed, often cripples the work of God. This is detrimental to the growth of the church.

More than once I have heard leaders from the church in China say, 'Please do not give us money. For money will divide the church.'

I challenge all of us to think beyond just money, for God's resources are more than this. In the global family of the body of Jesus Christ, many of us will bring different gifts. Some will bring a model of faithfulness in the context of suffering; some a model of perseverance in the context of poverty and injustice; some a model of godly leadership. Some will bring critical theological and missiological reflections and thinking, beyond the Western paradigm; some can share years of experience of commending the Lord Jesus Christ in the context of another world religion.

A one-directional giving is detrimental to the growth of the church.

As all of us contribute together, we will come to a fuller understanding of what it means to be the whole church bringing the whole gospel to the whole world. We must bring what we have, and not be bitter about what we don't have. Then we will rejoice in our diversity, as we listen and learn from our African brothers and sisters. We'll be dancing in that diversity! The time has already come, when the churches from the Global South are contributing significantly to world evangelization. Do we have the humility to receive their contribution joyfully, humbly and willingly? This sense of humility and unity in and under the Lord Jesus Christ will bring a sacrificial sharing of God's resources for world evangelization. That is the new equilibrium.

The redemptive purpose of God – reconciliation as the basis of our partnership

In 1979, when I read John Stott's *God's New Society* [now *The Message of Ephesians* in the Bible Speaks Today series], I was struck by the profound statement in the preface: 'For the sake of the glory of God and the evangelization of the world, nothing is more important than that the church should be, and should be seen to be, God's new society [community].'[3] This society, this new community, is characterized by reconciliation – reconciliation to God and to one another.

Reconciliation is the foundation of all Christian partnership. We need this reconciliation not only between ethnic groups, but between generations and between genders. It breaks my heart when senior leaders say to me, 'I'm going to quit, because I cannot understand the younger generation. And I am not accepted by them.' For the Spirit of Jesus is given to the whole church – God's new community includes those from the West and East, from the North and South, sons and daughters, young and old, men and women (Acts 2:17).

I was deeply humbled recently when I received news of a Japanese Christian woman. The lawyer informed me that she had passed away and had donated all her assets to the ministry of the gospel among the Chinese people. Now if we understand even a little bit of history, we'll understand the significance of this act of love. Reconciliation in Christ will always result in loving action for Christ. Many who were once enemies in the past because of ethnic and political conflicts are now serving together in the mission field, together bringing and proclaiming the gospel of reconciliation.

As we work and partner together, we must declare to the world the message of reconciliation. It will seem like foolishness, but as Chris Wright once said, 'The world is in a holistic mess, and in desperate need of a holistic gospel.' Partnership, founded on reconciliation and expressed in sacrificial and humble loving service, will speak powerfully.

So reconciliation is the foundation of partnership, and the cross is at its centre. The cross symbolizes death in obedience to God, and true biblical partnership requires each of us to die to self. It may be to die to our own ambitions, so that others may succeed, to our desire to be in key positions of influence, so that others may take the lead. It could be to die to our own opinions or to an insistence on how ministries should be run, so that others can be used by God for a greater work. When members of God's community all contribute sacrificially for the sake of the kingdom, equilibrium is possible.

True biblical partnership requires each of us to die to self.

It will come from the sanctifying work of the Holy Spirit, and be marked by submission to Jesus Christ, submission to one another, and death to self.

The danger of pride and self-pity

At the Edinburgh 1910 conference, there was such a strong desire to bring the gospel to the rest of the world, yet there were very few delegates from the younger churches in Asia, and hardly any from Latin America or Africa. By contrast, more than half of us at this Lausanne Congress today are from the Majority World. I rejoice in that. I rejoice too in the growth of the Asian church and in the growth of the Asian missionary movement. But I must say I also have a nagging restlessness and anxiety in me.

I hear many comments about twenty-first-century mission belonging to Asia, or belonging to the Chinese. But I'm concerned that many of us Asians may be repeating the same mistake that Western Christians made in the past: that is, equating economic and political power with advances in spreading the gospel. We continue to reinforce the notion that the spreading of the gospel is always from the powerful to the powerless, the haves to the have nots, and there is a sense of Asian triumphalism which makes me very nervous. I stand before you today and confess that I pray daily for myself, my people and the Chinese church, that Christ will keep us humble, and grant us mercy and grace.

The early church acknowledged the sovereign rule of God (Acts 4:24). He could even use kings like Pharaoh and Nebuchadnezzar: 'The Most High is sovereign over the kingdoms of men and gives them to anyone he wishes' (Daniel 4:17). No denomination, ethnic group or people can claim, 'We are the ones who will finish the Great Commission, hastening the Lord's return.' We have to work together. Professor Andrew Walls insightfully shared, 'There is no one, single centre of Christianity. Mission is from everywhere to everywhere.' Arrogance and self-pity will be the two major barriers to pursuing world evangelization.

The modern Protestant missionary movement of the last 200 years has had a rich heritage. We have many wonderful stories to tell, and to pass down, of the faith, love and hope of Western brothers and sisters who gave their lives for the sake of the gospel. And yet we need to tell new stories, of men and women from the global church, of Asians, Africans and Latin Americans, who similarly are passionate about reaching the lost with the love of Jesus Christ. But we *all* have a wonderful story to tell: the wonderful story of the gospel itself, the story behind all these stories. So let's keep on telling stories, new stories, as well as stories from the past.

Finally, partnership is a journey of friendship. The most influential speech of the 1910 Edinburgh conference was for me that of Samuel Azariah, an Indian leader. He said, 'In the generations to come, and through all the ages to come, the Indian church will rise up to give thanks for the missionaries. For their self-denying labours, you have fed the poor, you have given yourself to us, you have given your bodies to be burned. But we ask for one more thing: give us friends!'

I am grateful to God, as I stand before you, for the China Inland Mission, and for OMF, not because I serve with OMF, but for its leaders past and present. They have journeyed faithfully with me, and with many Asian brothers and sisters. We have developed a deep friendship. Without that, I could not be standing before you today. And I pray that out of this Lausanne Congress, there will be true, long-lasting, authentic friendships that will inspire us to partner in the body of Jesus Christ for world evangelization, to reconcile the world to God in Christ.

Patrick Fung, a medical doctor, serves as General Director of OMF International, formerly the China Inland Mission. www.omf.org

SCRIPTURE IN MISSION

Peter and Angela are busy with work, family, church and entertaining. They listen to political commentators on television and Christian talk-show hosts on the radio. They have at least ten Bibles in their home, but the only verses they ever hear read are those in the Sunday morning services. Their pastor expounds his own thoughts more than Scripture. The Scriptures, which used to occupy centre stage in their lives, have moved to the periphery, and family values are now set more by talking with friends than by engagement with the Bible.

Lucy and Julie live next door to Peter and Angela. Lucy's family emigrated from East Asia, and she is a Buddhist. Julie is interested in spirituality, New Age thinking, and the mystical elements in Buddhism and Hinduism. However, she believes Jesus rose from the dead and thinks this is 'cool'.

Mma Echu became a follower of Jesus a few years ago. There is no Scripture in her own language, and her pastor preaches in the dominant language of the nation, which she does not understand well, so she goes to church only occasionally. In her village, Chief Ekone built a shrine for his god next to his house, asking the god to protect and bless his family. He has heard of Jesus, but as far as he knows, Jesus speaks only the dominant language, not his language. There is no point in trying to enter into a dialogue on what Jesus says, for Jesus is a foreigner.

Amin, a shopkeeper, once heard about Jesus and now wants to learn more, but there is no-one to talk with. He once saw a book which people said was about Jesus, but he cannot read. He owns a radio and a DVD/CD player.

On the other side of town, living in a very different world, is Hussein, who is deaf. The deaf community fears the hearing community, as they have often been mistreated. No-one communicates about God to the deaf community. God is not just foreign to them; he does not exist.

Bible poverty

'Bible poverty' is universal. Its origin is found in the heart and in separation from God. Jesus said that we should love the Lord our God with all our heart, soul, mind and strength, and our neighbour as we love ourselves (Matthew 22:34–40; Mark 12:28–31). A life transformed by Scripture is pleasing to God and brings delight to our neighbours (1 Corinthians 13:4–7; Galatians 5:22–23; Ephesians 4:1–6, 25–32; Philippians 2:1–11; Colossians 3:12–17).

We need to work and pray for Scripture not only to be available, but to transform lives. We have two major hindrances at present: (i) where it is available, it is generally only in written form; (ii) over one billion people do not have adequate Scriptures in their own language.

The place of Scriptures in mission

The apostle Paul wrote to Timothy of Scripture's two key purposes: to make us wise about the way of salvation through faith in Jesus Christ, and to equip us for every good work as God's people (2 Timothy 3:14–17). Paul wanted his son in the faith to share the confidence he had, and that we can have, that the Scriptures are essential to sharing the gospel of Christ, and to experiencing Christ-like transformation.

It sounds as if Timothy's grandmother Lois, or his mother Eunice, read Scripture to him (2 Timothy 3:15). We learn in 2 Timothy 1:5 that their faith lived on in Timothy, who had known the holy Scriptures from infancy. These three people engaged with Scripture, and this led them to live with 'sincere faith' in a challenging society and culture.

Peter and Angela, Christians with several Bibles in their home, are biblically impoverished. When it comes to *engaging* with Scripture, their situation is not so different from that of Lucy and Julie, their neighbours, who know nothing of the Scriptures. Mma Echu and Chief Ekone do not have any Scripture in their own language, and so their Bible poverty is clearer. And Hussein is completely cut off until someone develops a way to communicate Scripture to him.

Where people have Scripture, they may be kept from engaging with it through ignorance, indifference and even contempt; through busyness or through preference for entertainment; through sensing Scripture's lack of immediate relevance; through philosophical questions about what can be known; or through a sense of humans being the autonomous centre of their own worlds.

Few Westerners now know anything about Scripture, and even if the Bible is familiar in a vague sense, it is not understood or valued. Many people, including Christians, are caught up with their responsibilities and activities. Peter and Angela do not see Lucy and Julie very often. They do not feel comfortable with Lucy's Buddhism or Julie's vaguely defined spirituality, but it would probably not occur to them to help their neighbours to calibrate their beliefs alongside scriptural truth. And if they *did* think of it, they wouldn't know how to do it, as no-one has ever taught them how. For Lucy and Julie, the Bible is merely 'strange', and it does not appear to be relevant to their lives.

The Western mindset

In Western culture, where Peter and Angela operate, we now see an historic shift in what a person can claim to know. Knowledge is regarded as less and less objective and increasingly subjective. What we *experience* of the external world is what counts, rather than what our reason tells us. What has been passed down as fact is now seen as mere opinion, or as the self-serving ideas of our elders, who want to train us to live in their society. Truth is no longer fixed, and there is no means to find it. Biblical truth, including biblical morality, is seen in the same light. So biblical truths, about the world or morality, are just opinions from an earlier era, with no universal claims on human beings.

The individual is the centre of his or her universe, deciding who is god and what is true, generalizing from a personal experience of reality. There is less and less trust in any external authority, whether civic authority, God or the Bible. In place of authority relationships, there are now just power games and matters of personal preference. The highest value is no longer love, but tolerance.

Finding bridges to spiritual understanding

The Spirit of God is the One who changes the condition of a person's heart, freeing it from the control of sin and freeing us to serve God (Romans 8:1–11). The Spirit is not limited or restricted by any context, but crosses all barriers. The Spirit, himself the great bridge, allows us also to establish bridges for others.

If ignorance is the problem, and the person is willing to learn, a good starting place is the larger narrative of the Scriptures, from creation through to the new heaven and new earth. The focus will be on God's love for us in Christ, who took on our humanity and invited all people into his kingdom through his life, death and resurrection. How could Peter and Angela come to value, and then learn to share, the grand overarching story of the Bible with Lucy and Julie?

If we meet with indifference, we can always share how the Scriptures have influenced us in our lives or in a decision or an action we took. We can talk of the larger narrative or more specific passages which have made a deep impact on us. Peter and Angela could learn how to show Lucy and Julie the relevance of spiritual truths in Scripture today. Taking biblical narratives or parables to do this can be particularly effective. Such sharing will demonstrate the personal relevance of Scripture.

If the person is contemptuous, we should press on, showing consistent love and praying for the work of the Spirit.

It is always worth considering the idea of bringing people together to encounter God's Word for themselves, as Rebecca Manley Pippert has recommended (see p. 50ff.). Meeting in a small group to investigate the Scriptures holds each person accountable to the others. The regularity of the discussion, perhaps weekly, encourages each person to keep thinking about the Scriptures in his or her own life. Each person hears the genuine questions others are asking, and the group members grow both together and individually.

If the barrier is philosophical or concerns questions that relate to what human beings can know, and if this is an area in which you are not skilled, you could find a book to lend, or consult a church leader who is familiar with Christian publishing, so that he or she can recommend one.[4]

More than a billion people have no Scriptures

There are approximately 6,900 languages (not including local dialects) spoken today.[5] Those spoken by smaller populations are called 'minority' languages, of which there are many. Of the total number of languages, some 94% are spoken by only 6% of the world's population (or about 400 million people). People like Mma Echu and Chief Ekone fall into that broad statistic.

Is it really acceptable that over a billion people do not have a complete Bible in their own language? If we believe in the importance of everyone having Scriptures in their own language, would we not expect church and mission leaders to come together to find ways to eradicate such Bible poverty? The human and financial resources already exist to change this. So what hinders it? Bible agencies cannot address this on their own. An effective response will require the input of the global church. How can we get past the over-reliance of churches and missions on Bible agencies?

About 450 of the 6,900 languages have a complete Bible.[6] These languages represent about 5 billion people. Of the remaining languages, nearly 2,000 have translation work in progress, over 2,000 have no translation yet underway,[7] and 1,510 have fewer than 1,000 speakers remaining:[8] some are nearly extinct; others too poorly researched for us to know the number of speakers. So in summary, over a billion people still do not have the whole Bible available.

Most minority-language communities are small, and can become marginalized in their nations. They are poor, not well endowed with social services, and have little place in the political structure.

People from minority languages often learn at least enough of the majority language to buy and sell in the market. Their ability to use the majority language in this way can mistakenly lead those from the majority culture – and from outside – to believe that they understand it well enough to read Scripture. But more research is needed into what languages are most suitable for use with minority-language speakers.

If more than one language is spoken in a region, we should identify the need for Scripture to be made available, and then work with churches and Bible agencies to develop a plan to meet that need. The plan should include training in how to teach Bible stories orally in the minority language.

If you cannot identify any languages spoken in a city or region, the nearest university with a research department in languages and culture will be a good source of information. Bible agencies working in the region can also provide useful information, and may have suggestions on a way forward.

Can Scripture be provided in more forms than print?

We commonly assume the Bible will be in written form. But does one have to be literate to be a Christian? Have we become satisfied with print because church leaders are literate? How do we serve the billions of people from oral cultures? Many have never needed to read; most are unable to do so. In addition, there are those who are deaf and blind who need special attention.

We should research the appropriate media and forms which will be most effective, using all technology available, for example, radio, audio (CDs, mp3 players), video, internet or cell phones. All can be media for oral Bible stories.

Scripture is God's truth for ever, and will never pass away. Let us work together to bring it to the whole world, for his glory.[9]

Written by the Scripture in Mission Resource Team[10]

MEN AND WOMEN IN PARTNERSHIP

Scripture affirms that God created men and women in his image and gave them dominion over the earth together. Sin entered human life and history through man and woman acting together in rebellion against God. Through the cross of Christ, God brought salvation, acceptance and unity to men and women equally. At Pentecost, God poured out his Spirit of prophecy on all flesh, sons and daughters alike. Women and men are thus equal in creation, in sin, in salvation, and in the Spirit.[11]

All of us, women and men, married and single, are responsible to employ God's gifts for the benefit of others, as stewards of God's grace, and for the praise and glory of Christ. All of us, therefore, are also responsible to enable all God's people to exercise all the gifts that God has given for all the areas of service to which God calls the church.[12] We should not quench the Spirit by despising the ministry of any.[13] Further, we are determined to see ministry within the body of Christ as a gifting and a responsibility in which we are called to *serve*, and not as a status and a right that we demand.

a) We uphold Lausanne's historic position: 'We affirm that the gifts of the Spirit are distributed to all God's people, women and men, and that their partnership in evangelization must be welcomed for the common good.'[14] We acknowledge the enormous and sacrificial contribution that women have made to world mission, ministering to both men and women, from biblical times to the present.

b) We recognize that there are different views sincerely held by those who seek to be faithful and obedient to Scripture. Some interpret apostolic teaching to imply that women should not teach or preach, or that they may do so but not in sole authority over men. Others interpret the spiritual equality of women, the exercise of the edifying gift of prophecy by women in the New Testament church, and the hosting of churches in their homes, as implying that the spiritual gifts of leading and teaching may be received and exercised in ministry by both women and men.[15] We call upon those on different sides of the argument to:

i. Accept one another without condemnation in relation to matters of dispute, for while we may disagree, we have no grounds for division, destructive speaking, or ungodly hostility towards one another;[16]
ii. Study Scripture carefully together, with due regard for the context and culture of the original authors and contemporary readers;
iii. Recognize that where there is genuine pain, we must show compassion; where there is injustice and lack of integrity, we must stand against them; and where there is resistance to the manifest work of the Holy Spirit in any sister or brother, we must repent;
iv. Commit ourselves to a pattern of ministry, male and female, that reflects the servanthood of Jesus Christ, not worldly striving for power and status.

c) We encourage churches to acknowledge godly women who teach and model what is good, as Paul commanded,[17] and to open wider doors of opportunity for women in education, service, and leadership, particularly in contexts where the gospel challenges unjust cultural traditions. We long that women should not be hindered from exercising God's gifts or following God's call on their lives.

The Cape Town Commitment IIF3

WE HAVE A GOSPEL TO PROCLAIM
Lindsay Brown

Therefore, since through God's mercy we have this ministry, we do not lose heart. Rather, we have renounced secret and shameful ways; we do not use deception, nor do we distort the word of God. On the contrary, by setting forth the truth plainly we commend ourselves to every man's conscience in the sight of God. And even if our gospel is veiled, it is veiled to those who are perishing. The god of this age has blinded the minds of unbelievers, so that they cannot see the light of the gospel of the glory of Christ, who is the image of God. For we do not preach ourselves, but Jesus Christ as Lord, and ourselves as your servants for Jesus' sake. For God, who said, 'Let light shine out of darkness,' made his light shine in our hearts to give us the light of the knowledge of the glory of God in the face of Christ.

But we have this treasure in jars of clay to show that this all-surpassing power is from God and not from us.
(2 Corinthians 4:1–7, read to the Congress, in Arabic, French and Spanish)

The gospel of Jesus Christ is unique, wonderful, powerful and true. It is the greatest message in the history of the world, and we want to share it with others. That is why we've been meeting together.

What do we hope will be the legacy of this Congress? What will we say when we return home?

Over the last year, Chris Wright and a team of theologians from around the world have been working on *The Cape Town Commitment*. Its two-part structure is based on our attempt to respond to Jesus' two commands: to love God and to love one another. It follows the style of Paul's letters, where he first outlines a series of doctrinal convictions and then spells out the implications of these beliefs for our lifestyle. In summarizing our doctrinal convictions, we are not attempting to be doctrinaire. In our judgment, it is important that each generation of believers reflects on and restates in a fresh way what they believe. I hope you will read it carefully and digest it. Our prayer is that it will be a help to many mission agencies, churches and Christian organizations around the world.

In the preamble, the authors list the legacy of the first and second Lausanne Congresses. Among the major gifts to the world church of the first Congress in 1974 were (i) *The Lausanne Covenant*, (ii) a new awareness of unreached people groups, and (iii) a fresh discovery of the holistic nature of the biblical gospel and of Christian mission. The second Congress gave birth to *The Manila Manifesto*, and to more than 300 strategic partnerships between nations in all parts of the globe.

What will be the legacy of this Congress? Only God knows – we don't, at this stage. But I can tell you the fourfold vision and the hope of the organizers.

Firstly and paramountly, for a ringing reaffirmation of the uniqueness of Christ and the truth of the biblical gospel, and a crystal-clear statement on the mission of the church – all rooted in Scripture. We cannot engage in mission unless we are clear on what we believe. Without a foundational commitment to truth, we have little to offer. The great missionary conference of Edinburgh 1910 set in motion huge missionary endeavour.

What will be the legacy of this Congress?

But it had one big flaw: the organizers sidelined doctrine. Recently John Stott told me he was ashamed that leaders in his own communion had refused to discuss doctrinal issues for fear of division. As a result, the Congress launched a movement without biblical consensus. As Stott said, 'You cannot speak of the gospel of Christ and the mission of the church without reflecting on biblical truth.' To attempt it is folly.

So we need to have clarity, especially on four things: (i) the exclusive claims of Christ; (ii) the meaning of Christ's death; (iii) the necessity of conversion; and (iv) the lostness of humankind. *The Cape Town*

Commitment seeks to give this clarity. It is effectively a statement of what evangelicals believe.

There is no need for us to be ashamed of this word 'evangelical'. It simply means 'people of the gospel'. It is not a new word, neither is it a Western word, nor a Reformation word. Nor is evangelicalism a sect. It has its roots in Scripture (*euangelion*) and was used amongst church leaders as early as the second century; for example, Tertullian used it in his defence of biblical truth against the heresies of Marcion. When we use the term, we are simply aspiring to articulate and communicate authentic and biblical Christianity. Lausanne is an unashamedly evangelical movement.

My first question to you is this: Did you hear this ringing affirmation, and do you agree with it?

Secondly, our vision and our hope was to identify key issues which the church needs to address seriously in the coming decade. The mission statement for this Congress was 'to seek to bring a fresh challenge to the global church to bear witness to Jesus Christ and all his teaching, in every part of the world – not only geographically, but in every sphere of society, and in the realm of ideas'. The phrase 'bear witness' is carefully chosen. In many ways, I think it is a better word than 'evangelization'. It is often translated from the Greek word *martyria* in the English Bible to imply both speech and behaviour, a witness of life and lip. We must be committed to the lordship of Christ in every area of human activity. I love the words of Abraham Kuyper, the Dutch theologian and prime minister, who once said, 'There is not one centimetre of human existence to which Christ, who is Lord of all, does not point and say, "That is mine".'

The evangelical church has rightly put an emphasis on reaching every nation and every people group with the gospel of Jesus Christ. That must not be diminished. We have, however, perhaps been a little weaker in our attempts to apply biblical principles to every area of society, for example to the media, business, government, public policy, the university . . . Charles Malik, the Lebanese statesman who led the UN General Assembly and fashioned the UN Declaration on Human Rights, asked, 'What does Jesus Christ think of the university?' What a question! He urged Christians to 'try to recapture the university for Christ', for, he said, 'Change the university, and you change the world.' Martin Luther had said much the same in 1523.

During this Congress, we have also been challenged to apply a Christian mind to ethical issues such as ethnicity and creation care, amongst others. We need to engage deeply with human endeavour and with the ideas that shape it. As Sir Fred Catherwood said, 'To wash your hands of society is not love, but worldliness; to engage in society is not worldliness but love.'

Many secularists have tried to persuade us to retain our faith only as a private matter and keep it out of the public domain. This would imply the Christian message is relevant only in our homes and churches, but not in society. That is not the teaching of the Bible. One of our hopes for this Congress is that we leave here (i) passionately committed to communicating the gospel to the ends of the earth, and (ii) equally committed to demonstrating that the eternal truths of Scripture apply to the whole of life. For Christ is Lord over the whole of creation. Affirming the lordship of Christ and attempting to develop a Christian mind will have three implications: it will (i) glorify our Creator; (ii) enrich our Christian lives; and (iii) enhance our witness.

My second question is this: Are you committed to bearing witness to Christ in every area of life?

Thirdly, our vision and our hope was that from this Congress will issue many fruitful partnerships. That's why such great care was taken with the formation of the small groups. Our hope was that, through them, many fresh friendships and partnerships would come into existence. In a needy and broken world, we cannot afford to be driven by a spirit of competition; such a spirit must give way to a spirit of partnership, where both men and women, as well as people of different ethnicities, join hands under Christ to communicate the gospel of Christ to the ends of the earth.

Such partnerships will need to transcend denominational and organizational divides. Our prayer is that many mission agencies working in the same field will, after the Congress, partner together to avoid duplication, competition and wastage. We need a new generation of evangelical statesmen and women who are driven by their commitment to the cause of Christ above all, and who genuinely rejoice, like Paul in Philippians chapter 1, when the gospel goes forth, no matter who is leading the charge. Our prayer has been that many of us would leave this place with a fresh commitment to partnership with other like-minded believers.

My third question is this: Are you thinking of fresh partnerships into which you can enter after this Congress?

Fourthly, our vision and hope has been that many new initiatives will issue out of this Congress. We maintain too much, and pioneer too little. How can we rest when millions have never heard the gospel? In 1974, there was a great surge of interest throughout the global church in unreached people groups. Who knows what will come from this Congress? Maybe there will be fresh initiatives in reaching oral learners, young people, diaspora or the cities. Who knows what new ministries the Congress will spawn? Maybe it will lead to fresh energy in communicating biblical truth in the public domain, in the media, the world of the arts, uni-

> **We maintain too much, and pioneer too little.**

versity and government, all of which shape the value systems in nations and require bold, clear and coherent Christian testimony.

My fourth question is this: What fresh initiatives will *you* take, coming out of this Congress?

Whatever God is pleased to do, I believe these verses in 2 Corinthians give us three principles to take away. These principles have been repeated throughout the Congress:

1. Mission is Christocentric

Our ministry, or calling, at its core, is to present the deity, incarnation, death, resurrection and lordship of Jesus Christ.

At the press conference today, a journalist asked me, 'Bishop Stephen Neill says that when mission is everything, mission is nothing. What is *not* the mission of the church?' My answer: 'When the church proclaims a message without the deity, incarnation, death, resurrection and lordship of Christ at its centre, that is not mission.'

Look at the way Paul highlights the following:

- Verse 4 – the light of the gospel of the glory of Christ who is the image of God
- Verse 5 – preaching Christ Jesus as Lord
- Verse 6 – the glory of God in the face of Christ

Our message is unashamedly Christocentric. When Sadhu Sundar Singh, the great Indian leader, was once asked what was so special about the Christian faith, 'Only Christ' was his reply. I once asked a Christian woman in north India, 'Why are you a Christian in a culture where the vast majority are Hindus and Muslims?' Her answer: 'I'm a Christian because it is only through Christ I can know God as my Father and have an intimate relationship with him; only through Christ can I know my sins forgiven; and only through Christ can I have the hope of eternal life.' He is not just *a* Saviour – but *the unique* Saviour of the world. He is not just one among many, but the *only* Lord and Saviour. He does not bear comparison with any other religious leaders. He is incomparable. Our calling is by *all* means to communicate this message to the world. Some will do it by preaching and proclamation, but all are called, according to the New Testament, to bear witness to him.

Some of us may engage in dialogue in the public sphere. It is amazing how creative the early evangelists were, speaking in local synagogues, and in neutral territory, as did Paul on Mars Hill. There is no substitute for engaging in Christ's commission to testify verbally to his lordship.

Our communion meal this evening focuses on John the Baptist's ecstatic claim when he saw Jesus and called him 'the Lamb of God who takes away the sin of the world'. When I was a student at Oxford University many years ago, I studied in the same college where John Wesley had been a professor 250 years previously. It

was a wonderful place to read the letters and sermons of Wesley.
I took the opportunity to read through
his journals which he recorded every   **'I offered**
day during his itinerant ministry. One   **Christ to the**
phrase struck me, repeated day after   **people.'**
day in his journals: 'I offered Christ to
the people . . . today I offered Christ to the people.' That is our
primary calling, to offer Christ to the peoples of the world.

2. The need for integrity

We are to watch our walk! Our words must come from godly lives.
We are called to bear witness to Christ as fallen, fragile people, or as
'earthen vessels' (verse 7). We should be careful about over-focusing
on technique or on clever approaches (verse 2); the gospel should
be shared not by craftiness or by adulterating the Word of God, but
out of our weakness (verse 7), focusing on the power of God.

There is no room for overconfidence or triumphalism. We dare not
say we will accomplish this task because we have the money and the
technology. Rather, the mission of taking the gospel to the ends of
the earth will be accomplished only because of the greatness of the
gospel, the power of God, the unique message of the saving Christ,
and the help and power of the Holy Spirit and the Word of God. As
we go out, we are to focus on the truth of the gospel (verse 2), the
gospel of the glory of God (verse 4), the lordship of Christ (verse 5),
the glory of God in the face of Christ (verse 6). But this word of truth
is to be backed up by authentic, transformed, joyful lives.

John Stott said in his last published sermon that the greatest
hindrance to the advance of the gospel worldwide was the failure
of God's people to live like God's people.

The teaching of the whole of Scripture is that we are to demonstrate godly lives before a watching world: lives which issue not just
in pious statements, but in compassion in a needy and broken world,
by caring for the underprivileged, the poor, those affected by
pandemics, the broken-hearted. It is intriguing to remember the
words of Adolph Harnack, the great German church historian, who

said that the two reasons why the primitive church grew were because they out-*argued* the pagans (articulating and defending Christian truth in public) and they out-*lived* them. These two things must come together. Jesus' approach was very simple. He spoke to the 5,000, and he fed them. So should we.

Our calling is to be morally distinct without being socially segregated. For those who are very word-centred, with a strong commitment to verbal communication of the gospel, our challenge is to balance this with empathy and care for the needy and broken. We must be careful to avoid the failings of the disciples who wanted Jesus only to speak to the 5,000 and then send them away. He would not allow that, and neither should we.

For those committed to ministries of compassion, empathy and care, our challenge may be to ensure that expressions of compassion are supported by taking every opportunity – graciously, sensitively, compassionately and wisely, but also verbally – to communicate the gospel of Christ. J. I. Packer is right when he says, 'A dumb Christian is a disobedient Christian.' So we must do both.

Earlier this week, Antoine Rutayisire gave us a wonderful biblical framework for a ministry of reconciliation which brought these two things together. He did not have time to share his own experience in his home country of Rwanda: how he saw his own father killed in front of him when he was only six years old, or how in his mid-thirties he lost all his co-workers in the IFES-related student ministry, killed because of their determination to stand against ethnic violence and demonstrate their unity in Christ across the ethnic divide. He was taken to a refugee camp with his pregnant wife, where he spent several months. I wrote to him from my home in Wales in 1994, offering to pay for him to come out of the country for a year's sabbatical to recover from the trauma. I'll never forget his reply. I still have the letter. He wrote, 'Thank you, Lindsay, for your kind invitation to come to Wales for a sabbatical. It is very attractive. However, when the way is open, I will return to the capital, Kigali. For if I do not share in my people's pain, neither can I share with them the joy of the gospel.'

A radical Christian lifestyle may require sacrificial commitment and service. Words may not be enough.

3. The call to perseverance

Finally, the apostle exhorts us not to lose heart (verse 1). In 1 Corinthians 15:58, he said, 'Be steadfast, immovable, always abounding in the work of the Lord, knowing that in the Lord your labour is not in vain.' Many of us will return to difficult circumstances, and may even entertain the possibility of giving up because the work is so hard. Such temptations can come more strongly when we return from the mountain-top experience of a Congress like this one. Then we are to remember our calling to persevere to the end and not lose heart or give up. I well remember at the last Lausanne Congress in 1989, talking with the only delegate from Somalia. He was employed by the United Nations to work in Mogadishu. He was the only Somali elder in the only evangelical church in the capital, made up of seventy believers. He had received an invitation to go and work with the UN in New York, but turned it down so that he could work among his own people. As a consequence, he lost his life in 1990, one year after the Congress. In that same Congress, Luis Palau had said that, if we were to gather in ten years' time, some would be absent because they had lost their lives in the Lord's service. That may well be true also of some of us here. Gospel service is costly, but we are to continue because of the glory of the gospel and the commission of our Lord.

Samuel Escobar, one of the grandfathers of The Lausanne Movement, said that the only thing twentieth-century man discovered was speed! We must have it and have it quickly! But Christian ministry is rarely like that. Often the work of God grows slowly. We thank God for rapid growth, but often the Word of God takes root slowly. We are to take a long view, not give up, and fulfil the ministry which God has given us. We are called, as Eugene Petersen said, to 'a long obedience in the same direction'. Before I close, let me give two illustrations of people who have done that.

One is Professor Jerry Gana, a senior politician in Nigeria, who has served five consecutive presidents, Muslim and Christian. Jerry has a reputation for remaining free of corruption. I once asked him how, in over thirty years of political life, he had managed to retain his reputation as a man of integrity and fairness. He said there were three factors:

1. He learned as a young student what it meant to abide in Christ and keep short accounts. We need to teach that too.
2. He chose his colleagues and partners slowly because, he said, even some Christian politicians make foolish mistakes. When you identify with a particular policy or an individual, if it all goes wrong, you have to face the consequences, and it can damage your testimony too.
3. He realized from early on the importance of legacy. He said,

> God has given me the privilege of serving in public life for thirty years. I hope I will be able to continue for another twenty-five. During that time, I'd like to mentor and develop a generation of young evangelical politicians in Nigeria. My hope and prayer is that they will go on and multiply that influence in their own generation; and that God will impact the political life of this nation through evangelical Christian politicians over a sixty-year period.

What a tremendous long-term vision and aspiration!

He realized the importance of legacy.

The second is Adoniram Judson, one of the early American missionaries. You may remember learning that he arrived in Burma, or Myanmar, in 1812, and died there thirty-eight years later in 1850. During that time, he suffered much for the cause of the gospel. He lost his first wife, Ann, to whom he was devoted, as well as several children. He was imprisoned, tortured and kept in shackles. Statistics are unclear, but there were only somewhere between twelve and twenty-five professing Christians in the country when he died; there were no churches to speak of, but he had completed the translation of the Bible just before his death.

Paul Borthwick spoke at the 150th anniversary of the translation of the Bible into the Burmese language. Just before he got up to speak, he noticed in small print on the first page the words: 'Translated by Rev. A. Judson'. So he turned to his interpreter, Matthew Hla Win, and asked him, 'Matthew, what do you know of this man?' Matthew began to weep. 'We know him – we know how he loved the Burmese people, how he suffered for the gospel because of us, out of love for us. He died a pauper, but left the Bible for us. When he died, there were few believers, but today there are over 600,000 of us, and every single one of us traces our spiritual heritage to one man: the Rev. Adoniram Judson.' But he never saw it!

And that will be the case for some of us gathered here. We may be called to invest our lives in ministries, for which we do not see much immediate fruit, trusting that the God of all grace who oversees our work will ensure that our labour is not in vain.

> Therefore, my beloved brothers, be steadfast, immovable, always abounding in the work of the Lord, knowing that in the Lord your labour is not in vain.
> (1 Corinthians 15:58)

Let me leave you with the words of John Wesley. As you seek to bear witness to Christ, 'With God's help: Do all the good you can, by all the means you can, in all the ways you can, in all the places you can, at all the times you can, to all the people you can, as long as ever you can', until Christ returns or calls us home. Let us all press on to the end in serving Christ, our King.

Lindsay Brown, former International General Secretary of IFES, is International Director of The Lausanne Movement, and IFES Evangelist-at-Large. www.lausanne.org www.ifesworld.org

The closing ceremony took the form of a special musical setting of the Kenyan service of Holy Communion. This was presided over by The Right Revd Henry Luke Orombi, Archbishop of Uganda and Honorary Chair of the Cape Town 2010 Africa Host Committee. The bread and wine were served around the hall using communion sets borrowed from a hundred local churches around the world, symbolizing the remembering of Christ's death in many nations.

APPENDIX:
The Lausanne Global Conversation

The Lausanne Global Conversation was initiated before Cape Town 2010 as an internet-based forum on the Congress issues. It continues today as a place where globally and locally mission leaders convene and connect around *The Cape Town Commitment*, through online discussions and sharing resources.

As a part of the conversation, *Christianity Today* magazine published a major article each month from October 2009 to October 2010, which was then carried by many other magazines and journals, in English and in several other languages. As we moved towards the Congress, the Lausanne Global Conversation was further developed through radio programmes, particularly across Africa and parts of Latin America.

As part of the conversation, Ajith Fernando was invited to write an article on embracing suffering. This article appeared in the August 2010 *Christianity Today*, and is reproduced here in full, together with a response from Elizabeth Little.[1]

Readers are invited to join the conversation at: www.lausanne.org/conversation

EMBRACING SUFFERING IN SERVICE
Ajith Fernando

I write this shortly after returning from a week of teaching pastors in the deep south of Sri Lanka. The experience of these pastors shows that, when people pioneer in unreached areas, it often takes ten to fifteen years before they see significant fruit and reduced hostility. In the early years, they get assaulted and accused falsely, stones are thrown onto their roofs, their children are given a hard time in school, and there are few genuine conversions. Many pioneers give up after a few years. But those who persevere bear much eternal fruit. I am humbled and ashamed of the way I complain, when I have problems that are so minute in comparison to theirs.

When I return from ministry in the West, my feelings are very different. I have been able to 'use my gifts' and spend most of my time doing things I like to do. I am hit by frustration when I return to being a leader in our less-efficient culture. The transition from being a speaker in the West to being a leader in Sri Lanka is a difficult one.

As a leader, I am the bond-slave (*doulos*) of the people I lead (2 Corinthians 4:5). This means that my schedule is influenced more by their needs than by mine. Vocational fulfilment in the kingdom of God has a very distinct character, quite different from vocational fulfilment in society. Jesus said, 'My food is to do the will of him who sent me and to accomplish his work' (John 4:34). If we are doing God's will, we are happy and fulfilled. But for Jesus, and for us, doing God's will includes a cross. The cross must be an essential element in our definition of vocational fulfilment.

Young Christian workers who come back to Sri Lanka after studying in the West struggle with this. They are highly qualified, but our poor nation cannot afford to give them the recognition that they think their qualifications deserve. They cannot use their gifts to the fullest because we cannot afford pure specialists. They struggle with frustration. Some end up leaving the country after a few years.

Some start their own organizations so that they can fulfil their 'vision'. Others become consultants, giving expert training and advice in their specialized field. Others pay the price of identifying with our people and ultimately have a deep impact on the nation.

I try to tell them that their frustration could be the means of developing penetrative insight. I try to explain that people like John Calvin and Martin Luther had a dizzying variety of responsibilities, so they could use their gifts only through tiredness. Yet the fruit of their labours as leaders and writers still blesses the church.

Frustration

Paul's theology afforded an important place to the need to endure frustration patiently, as we live in a fallen world awaiting the redemption of creation. Paul said that we groan because of this frustration (Romans 8:18–25). I believe we are not including this frustration in our understanding of vocational fulfilment today. A church that has a wrong understanding of fulfilment for its workers will certainly become a sick church. This may be one reason why there is so much shallowness in the church today. We have measured success by the standards of the world, and failed to challenge the world with the radically new biblical way to fulfilment.

> Luxuries became rights in the minds even of Christians.

The contemporary emphasis on efficiency and measurable results makes frustration even harder to endure. In the past four centuries, industrial and technological development in the West has resulted in efficiency and productivity becoming treasured values. With rapid economic development, things once considered luxuries became not only necessities, but also rights in the minds even of Christians. In this environment, the Christian's idea of commitment has taken a heavy battering.

We refer to our churches and Christian organizations as families, but families are very inefficient organizations. In a healthy family, everything stops when family members have big needs. We are often not willing to extend this idea of commitment to Christian body life.

Commitment

The biblical model of community life is Jesus' command to love
one another as he loved us – that is, for members to die for other
members (John 15:12–13). The model of Christian leadership is that
of the Good Shepherd dying for the sheep, without abandoning
them when the situation gets dangerous (John 10:11–15). When
God calls us to serve him, he calls us to come and die for the people
we serve. We don't discard people when they have problems and
cannot do their job properly. We serve them and help them to
overcome their problems. We don't tell people to find another place
of service when they rebel against us. We labour with them, until
we come to an agreement either to agree or to disagree.

When people leave a church because they did not fit into the
programmes, we communicate a deadly message: that our commitment is to the work one does and not to the person, that our unity
is primarily in the work and not in Christ and the gospel. The sad
result is that Christians do not have the security of belonging to a
community that will stay by them, no matter what happens. They
become shallow, never enjoying deep fellowship, and moving from
group to group. Churches can fulfil programmes and grow numeric-
ally in this way, but they don't nurture biblical Christians who
understand the implications of belonging to the body of Christ.

Sticking with people is frustrating because it is inefficient.
Spending hours listening to an angry or hurt person seems very
inefficient. Why should we waste time on that when there are professionals who can do it? So people have counsellors to do what their
friends should be doing.

Ideally, the counsellor helps to diagnose and treat difficult cases,
but friends devote the time needed to bring healing to hurting individuals, through acceptance, comfort and friendship. Hurt people
usually hurt those who try to help them. Hurt and angry people to
whom we are committed will hurt us too. Others who are hurt by
them could also get angry with us because we are committed to
those hurting people. But we endure that pain because Christ called
us to die for our friends.

Several people have sympathized with me, saying that it must be hard and frustrating to serve in a country wracked by war and hostile to evangelism. Indeed, we have suffered because of this. A few months ago, one of our staff workers was brutally assaulted, and he died. But I think the biggest pain I have experienced is the pain I have received from Youth for Christ, the organization for which I have worked for thirty-four years. Yet I can also say that, next to Jesus and my family, Youth for Christ has been the greatest source of joy in my life. Whether you live in the East or the West, you will suffer pain if you are committed to people. This is suffering that can be avoided. We can stop the relationship or move to something more 'fulfilling'. But then what do we lose?

Christ called us to die for our friends.

Some years ago, I was preparing a message on commitment while I was travelling in the West. Within the space of a few days, three people told me how they or someone close to them had left a group or a person because of problems they were having. One had left an unhappy marriage, another a church, and another an organization. Each of these was described as a merciful release from suffering. But I could not help asking myself whether, in each of these cases, the Christian thing to do would have been to stay and suffer.

Drivenness or servanthood?

I have a large group of people to whom I write asking for prayer when I have a need. Sometimes my need is overcoming tiredness. When I write about this, many write back saying they are praying that God would strengthen me and guide me in my scheduling. However, there are differences in the way friends from the East and some from the West respond. I get the strong feeling that many in the West think that, if one struggles with tiredness from overwork, that is evidence of disobedience to God. My contention is that it is wrong if one gets sick from overwork through drivenness and insecurity. But we may have to pay the price of tiredness, when we, like Paul, are servants of people.

The New Testament is clear that those who work for Christ will suffer because of their work. Tiredness, stress and strain may be the cross that God calls us to. Paul often spoke about the physical hardships his ministry brought him. This included emotional strain (Galatians 4:19; 2 Corinthians 11:28), anger (2 Corinthians 11:29), sleepless nights, hunger (2 Corinthians 6:5), affliction, perplexity (2 Corinthians 4:8) and toiling – working to the point of weariness (Colossians 1:29). In statements radically countercultural in today's 'body-culture' society, he said, 'Though our outer nature is wasting away, our inner nature is being renewed day by day' (2 Corinthians 4:16); and 'For we who live are always being given over to death for Jesus' sake, so that the life of Jesus also may be manifested in our mortal flesh. So death is at work in us, but life in you' (2 Corinthians 4:11–12). I fear that many Christians approach these texts with an academic interest, without seriously asking how they should apply them to their lives.

The West, having struggled with the tyrannical rule of time, has a lot to teach the East about the need for rest. The East perhaps has something to teach the West about embracing physical problems that come because of a commitment to people. If you think that it is wrong to suffer physically because of the ministry, then you suffer more from the problem than those who believe that suffering is an inevitable step along the path to fruitfulness and fulfilment. As the cross is a basic aspect of discipleship, the church must train Christian leaders to expect pain and hardship. When this perspective enters our minds, then pain will not touch our joy and contentment in Christ. I found eighteen different places in the New Testament where suffering and joy appear together. In fact, often suffering is a cause for joy (Romans 5:3–5; Colossians 1:24; James 1:2–3).

The glory of the gospel

In a world where physical health, appearance and convenience have gained almost idolatrous prominence, God may be calling Christians to demonstrate the glory of the gospel by being joyful and contented while enduring pain and hardship. People who are unfulfilled after pursuing things that do not satisfy may be astonished when they see Christians joyful and content after depriving themselves of these things for the sake of the gospel. This may be a new way to demonstrate the glory of the gospel to this hedonistic culture.

I have a great fear for the church. The West is fast becoming an unreached region. The Bible and history show that suffering is an essential ingredient in reaching unreached people. Will the loss of a theology of suffering result in the church in the West being ineffective in its evangelism? The church in the East is growing, and because of that God's servants are suffering. Significant funding and education come to the East from the West. With funding and education comes influence. Could Westerners be influencing Eastern Christians to abandon the cross, by sending a message that they must be doing something wrong if they are suffering in this way? Christians in both East and West need to have a firm theology of suffering, if they are to be healthy and fruit-bearing.

A SMALL VERSION OF
THE GRAND NARRATIVE:
A RESPONSE TO AJITH FERNANDO
Elizabeth Little

Thank you, Mr Fernando, for sharing your experience of suffering and personal frustration in service. I want to share from my own three decades of serving and raising a family in one of the most war-ravaged countries in the world.

For most Westerners, the opportunity to embrace suffering in service has become rare. Stringent security and evacuation protocols, government advisories, threats of litigation, and pressures from relatives and supporters make it difficult for missionaries working in conflict zones to live near to those who suffer. 'To stay, or not to stay?' is a relevant question for today's mission personnel working in dangerous places.

In today's world of instant access to news, mission agencies may feel compelled to 'do something' when danger arises. Although the Bible gives examples of varying responses to danger, the mission agencies' 'something', more often than not, may be to encourage or order an evacuation. What might have been a God-appointed time to embrace suffering and those who suffer may thereby be prematurely aborted.

According to a United Nations study, 'The World at War', increasing areas of the world are involved in 'intrastate' wars, where 75% of the victims are non-combatants. That figure represents a staggering story of human suffering and enormous needs.

I can remember two occasions when we and others stayed with people caught in conflict and suffering. On one occasion, we *had* to stay; it soon became too late to leave. On the other occasion, we had a choice, and we *chose* to stay.

The first occasion was in the late 1970s in a city where a dozen foreigners were living. My husband and I and our two daughters had been sent to complete the construction and opening of an eye hospital.

One March morning, rumours circulated that a citizens' uprising was brewing against the foreign political advisers who had been sent there to prepare for an invasion. We woke to the deafening blasts of government tanks firing on the crowds forming in the bustling open market, and jets strafing streets lined with mud-brick houses.

During a brief lull in the fighting, a military convoy was organized to take foreign advisers and government sympathizers to a safe place. We were offered a place in the convoy. Our neighbours, however, assured us the worst was over, so the convoy came and left without us. As the fighting worsened, and streets were abandoned, our neighbours fed us fresh bread and sweet milk. Some took turns guarding our gate, motioning angry mobs to pass by our home. When the fighting ended, they referred to us as 'the people who stayed'.

Months later, the hospital opened and we began preparing for Christmas. Not wanting to miss any chance for a party, our daughter invited her friends and their female relatives to a birthday event for Jesus. They packed themselves into our home to hear the Christmas story of Emmanuel, God with us. God blessed the painful times we experienced in that city.

The second occasion was in the country's capital during the mid-1990s. For months, opposing rebel forces fired rockets, sometimes a hundred a morning, into the streets. We were fewer than twenty foreigners, mostly medical personnel, and one child, our ten-year-old daughter. We lived in dark, sandbagged, first-floor rooms. Each morning we saw mounds of dirt piled outside our neighbours' houses, evidence of their attempts to dig makeshift underground shelters. We spread the word that we had a basement, and our neighbours were welcome there. Whenever rocketing began, they filed quickly through the gate and down the basement steps. With each incoming round of rockets, they moaned prayers and cried. In my own fearful state, all I could do was whisper the name of Jesus.

One of those women returned recently and told me that, during those basement times, whenever she heard the name of Jesus, she felt a warm sensation in her body. Later, when she left for a neighbouring country, she sought out Christians who could tell her more about the One who had warmed her heart. God blessed those days in the basement.

God blessed those occasions and visited us with his power. His amateur followers, stricken with stage fright, forgetting their lines, were acting out in miniature something of his own Grand Narrative – Emmanuel, God with us – in the miserable mess. The scenes set the stage for the Holy Spirit to work in a mighty way.

May the fruitful door of opportunity to embrace suffering in service, or at least embrace those who are suffering, remain open, for the sake of God's kingdom.

Elizabeth Little and her husband, Tom, have lived for thirty-two years in a war-torn country, working in medical assistance and training programmes.

[Editor's note: Shortly after Elizabeth Little wrote this response, she received news that her husband had been tragically murdered, while returning from a medical mission in a rural area.]

NOTES

Foreword

1. See 1 Chronicles 12:32.
2. *The Cape Town Commitment: A Confession of Faith and Call to Action* was drawn together by a global team of theologians under the leadership of Christopher J. H. Wright. It is available in the Didasko Files series (Lausanne Library/Hendrickson Publishers). For details of study guides and a graduate-level curriculum, see www.lausanne.org/books

Greetings from Billy Graham and John Stott to the Congress

1. All spelling and capitalization is as it appeared in the original greetings.

DAY 1. TRUTH: Making the case for truth in our pluralistic and globalized world

1. Other contributions on this theme may be found at www.lausanne.org/conversation
2. Cited in *The Guardian*, 23 September 2006.
3. Liu Xiaobo, *Tragedy, Aesthetic Judgment and Freedom*, published in Chinese (Taipei: Feng Yun Publishing Company, 1989), p. 74.
4. The Amsterdam 2000 gathering of evangelists from around the world was hosted by the Billy Graham Evangelistic Association.
5. Richard A. Posner, *Sex and Reason* (Cambridge MA: Harvard University Press, 1994).
6. 'Dover Beach' by Matthew Arnold was first published in 1867 in the collection *New Poems*.

7. Sir Fred Catherwood, *Light, Salt and the World of Business: Good Practice Can Change Nations*, Foreword by Paul Batchelor (Didasko Files: Hendrickson Publishers, 2011).

8. Some churches have, for example, introduced a regular slot in the service to ask a church member, 'What will you be doing at 10 o'clock tomorrow morning?' This helps the whole congregation to get a better grasp of what it means to be the church in the world, and expresses support for Christians, in whatever the Lord has called them to do.

9. Find more on Business as Mission at www.lausanne.org

DAY 2. RECONCILIATION: Building the peace of Christ in our divided and broken world

1. Editor's note: This paper was presented on behalf of an international advisory group. Its members include Claude Nikondeha (Burundi), Gerard Willemsen (Sweden), Joseph Nyamutera (Rwanda), Joyce Dube (Zimbabwe/South Africa), Menna Machreth (Wales), Nyasha Manyua (Zimbabwe), Peter Nyende (Kenya), Philbert Kalisa (Rwanda), Prabu Deepan (Sri Lanka), Rhiannon Lloyd (Wales), Solomon Sule-saa (Ghana) and Tito Paredes (Peru).

2. Genesis 10:5: 'From these the maritime peoples spread out into their territories . . .'.

3. Genesis 10:4; cf. 10:20, 31, 32.

4. Gordon J. Wenham, *Word Biblical Commentary, Volume 1: Genesis 1 – 15* (Waco: Word Books, 1987), pp. 216–217.

5. For a good analysis of the passage in Deuteronomy 2, see Christopher J. H. Wright, *New International Biblical Commentary: Deuteronomy* (Carlisle: Paternoster, 1996), p. 36. Some other passages that make the same point are Deuteronomy 26:19; Job 12:23; Psalms 22:27–28; 47:8; 86:9; Daniel 12:1; Acts 17:26–28.

6. Ibid., p. 133.

7. See also Isaiah 60:1–11.

DAY 3. WORLD FAITHS: Bearing witness to the love of Christ among people of other faiths

1. In this section all italics in Scripture are added for emphasis by John Piper.

2. This summary is drawn from 'Witness, Testimony', in Colin Brown (gen. ed.), *New International Dictionary of New Testament Theology*, vol. 3, translated with additions from *Theologisches Bergriffslexikon zum Neuen Testament*, A. A. Trite (Paternoster, 1976).

3. See John Stott, commenting on Titus 3:1–8, in *The Message of 1 Timothy and Titus*, Bible Speaks Today series (Leicester: Inter-Varsity Press, 1996).

4. Ibid., commenting on Titus 2:9–10.

5. John Stott, *The Lausanne Covenant: Complete Text and Study Guide* (Didasko Files: Hendrickson Publishers, 2011).

DAY 4. PRIORITIES: Discerning the will of God for evangelization in our century

1. Attempts were made to obtain written permission to publish an extract from 'Imagine', but were unsuccessful.

2. Lindsay Brown, *Shining Like Stars: The Power of the Gospel in the World's Universities* (Nottingham: IVP, 2007), pp. 133–134.

3. See 'The Future of Cities', *Financial Times*, 7 April 2010 (http://www.ft.com/cities), and 'The Global Cities Issue', *Foreign Policy Magazine* 181, Sept/Oct 2010 (http://www.foreignpolicy.com/articles/2010/08/11/the_global_cities_index_2010).

4. Parag Khanna, 'Beyond City Limits', *Foreign Policy Magazine* 181 (2010).

5. 'The Brown Revolution', *The Economist*, 9 May 2002.

6. Dorothy L. Sayers, *Why Work? An Address Delivered at Eastbourne, April 23rd, 1942* (London: Methuen, 1942).

7. For a paper by Paul Batchelor (UK) and Steve Osei-Mensah (UK/Ghana), see www.lausanne.org/conversation

8. For 'the university is a clear-cut fulcrum with which to move the world. The church can render no greater service to itself and to the cause of the gospel than to try to recapture the universities for Christ. More potently than by any other means, change the university and you change the world.' Charles Habib Malik, former President of the UN General Assembly, in his 1981 Pascal Lectures, *A Christian Critique of the University*.

DAY 5. INTEGRITY: Calling the church of Christ back to humility, integrity and simplicity

1. Charles Colson, *God of Stones and Spiders: Letters to a Church in Exile* (Illinois: Crossway, 1990), p. ix.
2. Elisabeth Elliot: *The Journals of Jim Elliot* (Grand Rapids, MI: Revell, 1978), p. 106.
3. A reference to an upcoming separation of Sudan into two nations.
4. Jacques Ellul, *Money & Power* (Downers Grove: IVP, 1984).
5. Ephesians 5:31–32; 2:15.

DAY 6. PARTNERSHIP: Partnering in the body of Christ towards a new global equilibrium

1. One unique aspect of the Congress was to have remote participation in over 600 sites, in ninety-three countries. Each Cape Town GlobaLink site arranged meetings throughout the week. Congress sessions were broken into segments and, together with a synopsis in multiple languages, uploaded to servers based in the US. Remote participation hinged on two elements: a robust internet connection to receive material and the successful uploading of that material.

On 17 October at approx 7:30 pm, thirty minutes after the start of the opening ceremony, all Lausanne websites ceased to function. It took until late the next morning to determine that this was due to a 'denial of services' cyber attack (i.e. saturating a website with external requests, such that it could not cope). In addition, a virus was introduced into the Convention Centre, causing the network and internet connections to slow to the point that video materials could not be uploaded to external servers. The attack was calculated and sophisticated.

The solution came when two cousins, computer experts from India and volunteers behind the scenes, identified the nature of the attack. One had just completed a doctorate in computational biology, covering the precise means employed. While the virus continued to make the system sluggish, videos could now be uploaded, using an internet connection several miles away from the Convention Centre. Despite these attempts to thwart communications, GlobaLink sites worldwide continued to meet, to discuss Congress issues and feed in responses.

2. A comprehensive overview of strategic priorities in world evangelization by Paul Eshleman (Vice President of Cru [formerly Campus Crusade for Christ] and Chair of the Lausanne Strategy Working Group, on whose behalf the paper is written), entitled 'World Evangelization in the 21st Century: Prioritizing the Essential Elements of the Great Commission' is available on the Lausanne website. This paper, together with *Operation World* and the *Atlas of World Christianity*, gives a clear overview of the task before the church now.

3. John Stott, *The Message of Ephesians: God's New Society*, Bible Speaks Today (Leicester: IVP, 1991).

4. For example, Chris Sinkinson, *Confident Christianity: Conversations that Lead to the Cross* (Nottingham: IVP, 2012), or Andrew Wilson, *If God, Then What? Wondering Aloud about Truth, Origins and Redemption* (Nottingham: IVP, 2012).

5. See the Ethnologue at www.ethnologue.com and select 'Browse the Web Version' and then 'Statistical Summaries'. See also the site of Wycliffe Bible Translators International: www.wycliffe.org/About/AssociatedOrganizations/WycliffeGlobalAlliance.aspx and select 'Translation Statistics'.

6. See the United Bible Societies at www.biblesociety.org

7. See www.wycliffe.org/About/AssociatedOrganizations/WycliffeGlobalAlliance.aspx

8. See the Ethnologue at www.ethnologue.com

9. Interact with this paper at www.lausanne.org/conversation Recommended reading: Harriet Hill and Margaret Hill, *Translating the Bible into Action: How the Bible Can Be Relevant in All Languages and Cultures* (Carlisle: Piquant Editions, 2008).

10. Michael G. Bassous (Bible Society of Lebanon); the late John Bendor-Samuel (formerly Wycliffe International and Forum of Bible Agencies International); Lucia Cheung (Scripture Union, Hong Kong); Ravi David (IFES, South Asia); Lloyd Estrada (Wycliffe Bible Translators, Asia); Richard Luna (One Hope); Fergus Macdonald (formerly United Bible Societies and Forum of Bible Agencies International); Michel Kenmogne (Cameroon Bible Translation and Literacy Association); Todd Poulter (Wycliffe Bible Translators International); Saju George

John (New Life Computer Institute); Sun-Chang Kwon (Wycliffe Bible Translators International); Naomi Swindon (Scripture Union, Australia); Chantal Tehe-Boa (IFES, Francophone Africa); Erní Walter Seibert (Brazil Bible Society); John Watters (Forum of Bible Agencies International).

11. Genesis 1:26–28; Genesis 3; Acts 2:17–18; Galatians 3:28; 1 Peter 3:7.

12. Romans 12:4–8; 1 Corinthians 12:4–11, Ephesians 4:7–16; 1 Peter 4:10–11.

13. 1 Thessalonians 5:19–21; 1 Timothy 4:11–14.

14. *The Manila Manifesto*, 1989: Affirmation 14.

15. 1 Timothy 2:12; 1 Corinthians 14:33–35; Titus 2:3–5; Acts 18:26; 21:9; Romans 16:1–5, 7; Philippians 4:2–3; Colossians 4:15; 1 Corinthians 11:5; 14:3–5.

16. Romans 14:1–13.

17. Titus 2:3–5.

Appendix

1. In May 2011, the Evangelical Press Association awarded this article first place (devotional category) in the Higher Goals Awards.

RECOMMENDED READING

The Mission of God, Christopher Wright (InterVarsity Press)
Portraits of a Radical Disciple, edited by Christopher Wright
    (InterVarsity Press)
John Stott: Pastor, Leader and Friend Christopher Wright et al.
    (Hendrickson/Lausanne Library. Didasko Files)
Light, Salt and the World of Business, Fred Catherwood (Hendrickson/
    Lausanne Library. Didasko Files)
An Authentic Servant, Ajith Fernando (Hendrickson/Lausanne Library.
    Didasko Files)
The Glory of the Cross, James Philip (Hendrickson/Lausanne Library.
    Didasko Files)
The Grace of Giving, John Stott (Hendrickson/Lausanne Library.
    Didasko Files)

The Cape Town Commitment

Text with brief overview questions (Hendrickson/Lausanne Library.
    Didasko Files series)
Study Edition, including full text, Rose Dowsett (Hendrickson/
    Lausanne Library)
Churches' curriculum for adult Sunday schools (Hendrickson/
    Lausanne Library)
Women's curriculum for personal and group use. See www.lausanne
    .org/se/about/resources/library.html
Graduate-level teaching curriculum (150 pp. annotated bibliography).
    See www.lausanne.org/se/about/resources/library.html

The Lausanne Covenant

Full text and study guide, John Stott (Hendrickson/Lausanne Library.
    Didasko Files)

Study Ephesians with the global church

Inductive Bible study/DVD for church fellowships, Lindsay Olesberg
    (Hendrickson/Lausanne Library)

.